Mamas Write

29 Tales of Truth, Wit, and Grit

by the
Write On Mamas

Edited by Janine Kovac,
Joanne Hartman,
and Mary Hill

BITTERSWEET PRESS
Oakland, California

Published by Bittersweet Press
Oakland, CA 2014
All rights reserved.

Edited by
Janine Kovac, Joanne Hartman, and Mary Hill
Design by Norma Tennis
Cover concept by Claire Hennessy

FIRST EDITION

978-0615964843

Cover image courtesy of Mary Allison Tierney

Printed in the United States of America

10 9 8 7 6 5 4 3 2 1

For our families—
who inspire us with the mundane and the sacred
and allow us to capture it all

Contents

Foreword

Kate Hopper

A YEAR AND A HALF AGO, I SAT ON ONE SIDE OF A LARGE, cobbled-together square of tables in the sunlit loft of the O'Hanlon Center for the Arts in Mill Valley, California. Women lined the periphery of the square and spilled onto the uncomfortable-looking couches against the wall. I was there to lead an afternoon writing workshop for the Write On Mamas.

We talked about character development and concrete details, and I gave them a writing prompt. Soon the sound of fingers tapping on keyboards and pens scratching across paper filled the room. And I could feel the energy bubbling up around me, an energy born when people write together.

I knew that some of these women wrote in order to document their lives, to not forget. Others were using writing to make sense of the world in which they were living, to find joy in what *is* rather than dwell on *what might have been.* Others wrote because they simply couldn't imagine not putting pen to paper.

When one by one they shared what had emerged from the writing exercise, I listened to their beautiful words spill out, words that described the textured, complex realities of their lives. And as always, I felt grateful, my understanding of humanity swelling, expanding.

I gave them another writing prompt, they once again bent their heads over their work, and I leaned back in my chair and smiled. My journey to that classroom began a decade ago with the premature birth of my daughter, who is now a healthy ten-year-old. My story was born out of fear and uncertainty, and writing it helped me plant my feet firmly on the ground once more. It led me to these women and to others like them.

That day in Mill Valley I knew that the Write On Mamas would send their words out into the world and change the world, reader by reader, because that is what good writing does. And they *have* sent their words out into the world—you are holding them in your hands.

Mamas Write examines the things that drive us to the page both as readers and writers. Some of these women (and one man) write to remember and create permanence, others to heal and transform. Some write to encourage, to make other mamas feel less alone. Others write and read to gain perspective, to understand what they think and believe.

This book was born from the common denominator that is motherhood, and these pieces tap into the urge to create, an urge that leads many a woman both to the delivery room and the blank page. But these essays are about much more than why mamas write. These writers are grappling with universals: love, acceptance, disappointment, grief.

And this anthology not only celebrates why and how and what these mothers are getting down on the page; it celebrates community, the ways in which we support each other as writers and as parents. In "The Next Prompt," the first piece in this book, Janine Kovac writes, "I know that if I can't share these feelings here—with these mothers who graciously share their stories with me—then [. . .] I will never write truthfully about anything."

These writers have taken a leap—to write their truth, and to share that truth with each other, to share it with you. This collection is ultimately about the power inherent not only in writing, but in sharing our stories. It's about creating a space— virtual or in person—where we all feel safe enough to be vulnerable, to write what we've been too scared to write.

So dive in, join the community. And when you're done reading the words in this book, pick up your pen and get your own truth down on the page. You won't be sorry.

Kate Hopper is the author of *Ready for Air: A Journey Through Premature Motherhood* and *Use Your Words: A Writing Guide for Mothers.*

Mamas Write

The Next Prompt

Janine Kovac

I ALWAYS SIT AT THE CARD TABLE, MY TUESDAY MAKESHIFT writing desk. Rachel and Angelisa share the big couch while Mary and Jill squeeze together on the little grey foldout couch from IKEA. Aluminum laptops emerge from tote bags. Cords are plugged in. A pitcher of dusty-pink herbal tea sits on the coffee table surrounded by coffee cups. A prompt is given (Rachel prepares them ahead of time). The timer is set for twelve minutes. (That's always my task.) Then we write. When the timer goes off we take turns reading aloud, always without comment. Then Rachel gives us another prompt and we start again. We write for two hours. Every Tuesday.

My friends write about their challenges: a blended family, a son with a genetic disorder, a baby who died when he was ten days old. They write about what it feels like to have a child in the hospital.

Sometimes I write about my challenges: a daughter who hates swimming lessons, twins who have suspected hearing problems or the husband who thinks he can live on raspberry iced tea and Pop-Tarts. But mostly I write to make my friends laugh. I write absurd stories in which Dick Cheney takes yoga classes in the Berkeley Hills but won't remove his black knee-high socks. I write about a family of raccoons who conspire to play practical jokes on a poodle in the neighborhood.

Occasionally I drift into memoir and write about my twins, who were due in April but born months earlier in December. I write in a distant voice, the way an alien might record life on Earth. I describe the proactive scenes—me, kneeling in front of the mirror for each of the ninety-two mornings the twins spent in the newborn intensive care unit and carefully applying the makeup I normally saved for parties before donning the brightest colors I could find in my closet. But I never describe the scene before that—me, dragging myself out of bed, trying to slough off despair and uncertainty.

I never venture past the bare facts. I've never tried to speculate as to why my husband stopped shaving the day I went into the hospital the week before Christmas and didn't shave again until his sons were discharged the week of Easter. When I write about my daughter, I record her precocious anecdotes rather than the months when she'd scream, "Mommy, don't leave me!" when I'd try to take a shower. If I write about the early diagnostic appointment during which the doctor told me to "expect to have a dead baby at every ultrasound," I transcribe her cold remarks but I don't write how I felt when I heard them.

The surface-level snippets I write on Tuesday mornings become prepared statements such as, "It really was a fifteen-minute surgery"—stock answers to family and friends who ask about our time in the NICU.

"How awful!" people say. Or, "You're handling this so we-ell!" And, "You're so strong not to cry!"

It's funny how emotional detachment gets mistaken for emotional strength. And even though I know the difference, I don't know how to digest our traumatic time in the NICU. I don't have the words to describe what those months felt like. So on Tuesday mornings when do I venture to write these detached scenes, I'm grateful that nobody asks me anything. My friends nod slowly or sigh deeply but they give me the space they intuitively sense that I need.

We write. I time. We read. I listen.

The other mothers write about their babies' fingers and toes, the smell of soft, downy hair, the textures of rich, creamy milk, of blue lips and limp limbs. I listen to Angelisa write about singing to her baby as he passes from this world into the next and the friend who brings her soup when she is too depressed to get up from the couch. I listen to Mary, who writes directly to her son, as if she were writing him a letter.

I watch as they crack open their hearts and read, never apologizing for their vulnerability. Only apologizing because they haven't written more. We cry as we listen. Eventually I put out a box of Kleenex next to the pitcher of tea.

Then one Tuesday, something changes. It starts out like any other busy morning. Nine-thirty a.m. and among the five of us we've already been to one physical therapy appointment, placated a feverish husband, arranged for two back-up sitters, dropped off a car for an oil change, and purchased a birthday cake. We've fielded calls from an insurance company, a special-education lawyer, a Realtor, and a seventh-grader who forgot her lunch. One by one we take our places in my living room.

"Ready?" Rachel looks around the room. I set the alarm on my phone for twelve minutes. She gives a benign-sounding prompt: "It is time to . . ."

"It is time to write," I think. But I type: "It is time to feel." The image that comes to mind is of me lying in my hospital bed a few hours after my emergency C-section. I'm holding photographs the nurses took of my baby boys. I wouldn't see them for another fourteen hours, but I didn't know that at the time, lying on the bed, woozy from medication and nauseous from the anesthesia.

I think past the thoughts that I had wanted to be true ("this is what a healthy one-and-a-half-pound baby looks like") and the thoughts I had spoken aloud to my husband ("this is a face only a mother could love") and let myself feel the fear of that moment—what I really saw in those pictures. Remembering feels like sticking needles under my fingernails. Pushing the memories aside makes the pinpricks go away. Nobody is making me write down my painful memories. Nobody expects me to pour my heart out. I could always just write about the raccoons. There are eleven more minutes to write before we get a new prompt.

I look at my flashing cursor. I know that if I can't share these feelings here—with these mothers who graciously share their stories with me—then I will never write truthfully about our time in the NICU. I will never write truthfully about anything.

I type what I see: "My baby's skin looks slimy, like a raw chicken breast." I look at it there on my screen, standing alone. I don't feel the pinpricks anymore; I just feel proud, as if something poisonous is now out of my system.

I record details about the boys' faces, such as the tape that held their breathing tubes in place and the eerie blue light that made them look as if their bruises had healed. I remember the helplessness of seeing my children hooked up to strange, life-giving machines. Each time I see a new vivid image I feel the needles again, but I keep typing anyway.

Letting myself remember is like guiding myself down the cold tunnels in the New Mexico caverns I'd visited as a child.

It's icy and the air feels thin, ancient, devoid of life, like the air in outer space. There's a path but it's too dark to see it. It feels as if I am the only person who has ever traveled here. And then I turn the corner and see something beautiful—ancient stalactites and mounds of limestone stalagmites—and realize I can't possibly be the only person to ever come here. There's no way someone could see such exquisite sparkling in the middle of pitch-black darkness and not be moved to share what they've experienced. Beauty such as this is meant to be shared.

I type until the timer chimes.

When it's my turn to read aloud, I pause in the middle of my sentences, as if they are confessions rather than memories. This is the easy part, I remind myself. The hard part was letting myself write it down in the first place. Or maybe the hard part was trying to keep it inside. My voice rises in pitch as I read. It's like an air bubble rising to the surface of the office water cooler. It cracks; I sob. Jill hands me a tissue and takes one for herself.

I had always pictured sharing sad news like flying artillery. But my friends react to my story the same way I react to theirs: softening, as if they are absorbing the blow rather than defending against it.

When I'm done, the room exhales.

Rachel whispers, "You're going there, Janine! You're finally writing about this! Good for you."

We wipe our faces. I blow my nose.

Then Rachel reads the next prompt.

Janine Kovac is an event coordinator with Litquake, San Francisco's annual fall literary festival. She is also a founding member of the Write On Mamas. Her work has appeared in Salon.com, fiction365.com, and in the anthology *Nothing But the Truth So Help Me God: 51 Women Reveal the Power of Positive Female Connection.* She blogs about her experience as a NICU mom for the science-based parenting site Raising Happiness and is an alumna of the Squaw Valley Community of Writers and Lit Camp. When not writing about preemies, Janine reads about fairies, dinosaurs, and garbage trucks. She lives in Oakland, California, with her husband and their three small and surprisingly noisy children.

The Write Identity

Jennifer Van Santvoord

LAST YEAR AT A COCKTAIL PARTY A HANDSOME STRANGER asked me, "So what do you do?" He was standing a little too close, though before marriage and kids, he would have been standing exactly where I wanted him.

Um, what? What do I do?

I panicked.

I started to sweat. *Oh no, can he see me sweating? No, of course not. That would be weird. He can totally tell that I'm a mom, can't he? It's like a giant poop stain all over the front of my dress. Wait, is there a poop stain on my dress? That wouldn't be so unusual. Likely, actually. But he can't seem to tell that I'm married. Personal space, buddy. Personal space.*

I'd been a stay-at-home mom for five years. *How do I make that sound sexy?*

I waited too long to respond. The silence between us was becoming awkward. He cocked his head to the side, almost like he thought there was something wrong with me. *There is nothing wrong with me, Mr. Handsome. I'm just not as quick to come up with a witty response to your sweat-inducing question since having children. Those little rug rats stole all my brain cells and never gave them back.*

Oh no! Say something!

I took a deep breath. "Well," I said slowly, "I'm at home with my kids for right now . . . and . . . um . . . I write a blog."

"What's the blog about?" he asked in a husky voice, as if hoping I would say something like, "Well, it's like *Fifty Shades of Grey* meets *Striptease*. You wanna get out of here?"

"It's about funny parenting stories, you know, that sort of thing," I said, almost apologetically. *Sorry to disappoint you, Mr. Handsome.*

He stared back at me blankly, and then I saw the look. His eyes started to glaze over. *He thinks I'm a joke. He definitely thinks I'm a joke.* It was a look full of what I'm sure could only be judgment and condescension.

Sigh. I'm such a cliché.

I am a mom who blogs, a "mommy blogger" as they say. Mommy bloggers are everywhere these days, making me feel a bit like a dime a dozen. But the truth is, as clichéd as I may feel, and may in fact be, writing has made me a happier stay-at-home mom.

Before babies and blogging, I was a career-driven woman. A woman who made her own money, had been her own person, her own boss, the master of her domain. My career was in sales. I sold meetings, events, and guest rooms to some of the biggest names in finance, and I was good at my job. I worked in some of the most well-known hotels in the world, donning stilettos and pearls and schmoozing with New York's elite financial community. I was important. Successful. Accomplished.

But I was also miserable.

I have a distinct pre-motherhood memory of watching a neighbor in my building walking up the stairs with her nine-month-old daughter at ten in the morning. She was wearing pajamas. I was wearing an uncomfortable black suit with nylons that were digging into my calves, and I thought, "Wow, I want that. I want what she has." She seemed so happy. So carefree. And I felt so trapped. Putting on a suit and working in a stuffy hotel every day, twelve hours a day, was suffocating me. I wanted out. The life she had seemed exactly what I needed. Comfy pajamas! Cute babies! Yes, this was for me!

So when my first child, Jackson, was born, I traded my stilettos for sweatpants and my pearls for poop-stained pj's.

A year later I found myself thinking, "Why did I want this?"

The truth was, I wasn't really sure why I wanted to be a stay-at-home mom. Sure, I enjoyed spending time with my son. I wanted to be the one to witness all his firsts, and all his other victories in between. And I was there. I was there the first time Jackson rolled over, the first time he sat up, crawled, and took his first steps. Not being there was not an option. And because I didn't enjoy my former career and was fortunate enough financially that I didn't have to go back to work, it just kind of worked out that way. But that wasn't the whole story; I am also such a control freak that I could not allow someone else to watch my son while I worked. I simply did not want someone else raising my child.

So I stayed home with Jackson. But even though there were periodic moments of joy, this new line of work was, for the most part, mind-numbing. And I wasn't even getting paid for it! I started having feelings of inadequacy as a contributor to my family, as a wife, and ultimately as a person, all because I was not working. My husband would come home from work and I would be in tears. He wanted to help me but he wasn't sure how. "Maybe you should go back to work then, if that is what will make you happy." Through sobs of frustration I would yell, "Well, what would I do?!! I didn't like what I was doing before, and I'm certainly not going to leave Jackson with some stranger so I can go do something I hate!"

But I knew I needed to do something, something for me, something I enjoyed outside of being a mom. I decided that starting my own business would be the answer. Photography was a passion of mine, and since Jackson had been born, I had begun experimenting with it a bit more. A friend encouraged me to use my skills as a photographer to create a unique brand of art for children's rooms. So I started photographing iconic letters from all over New York City, and used those letters to spell children's names, create alphabet prints, T-shirts, etc. It was a lot of fun, and I really enjoyed the process of creating both the business and the art from scratch.

I quickly realized that I needed to do something to promote it, and it seemed that everyone with a business was blogging. Because my business was kid-focused, it seemed only natural to write about children and parenting, something in which I was immersed. They say (whoever "they" is) that you should write what you know. So that is exactly what I did. I wrote about getting pooped on and getting peed on, food throwing and throwing up, Jackson saying "fuck" when he was learning to say "firetruck," Jackson asking me how he was "made" and what we "used" to make him, and on and on. And the more I wrote, the more I laughed and the better I felt about everything.

I realized that I really loved writing, loved finding humor in the everyday, often mundane tasks of motherhood. Writing simply made me feel better about myself.

So when my daughter Ella was born a year later, and my "free time" was reduced even more dramatically, the focus of my non-mom endeavors shifted from being centered on the creation of a business to being centered on writing.

Writing makes me feel like someone other than "just a mom" all day long. Not only am I (as my mom reminds me) keeping an invaluable record of my kids' childhoods, I am also maintaining my sanity by finding humor in situations that would otherwise make me cry, and then writing about them in a way that, instead, makes me laugh. When we moved from New York to San Francisco and my daughter screamed for five and a half of the six hours we spent flying to our new home city, and when six months later she threw up five times on our flight back to New York for the holidays, I had to write about it. I had to find humor in it. It was a means of survival, so that I didn't run off to Mexico by myself with no forwarding address. Writing became cathartic for me, a way to deal with the challenges of today while giving me the strength to face tomorrow. But still, I didn't consider myself a "writer"; I was just a blogger, trying to document a very important time in my family's life.

But then a couple of months later I attended a writing seminar. It was the first time I had ever been to a writing class, or a writing anything for that matter. For the previous four years I had just been writing for the sake of writing, writing to make it through the day. At the start of class the teacher quoted from a book called *Writing Alone and With Others,* by Pat Schneider: "A writer is someone who writes", the teacher said. When I heard those words, my first thoughts were: "Really? Me, a writer? Can I call myself that when all I do is write a little blog for my family, friends, and a handful of strangers? I don't even get paid for it." In the days that followed, I kept thinking about that quote. It was so simple, yet so powerful.

A writer is someone who writes. Huh.

Those six little words changed everything for me. That meant I was a writer. This was a revelation! I wasn't just another mommy blogger, and I wasn't just a mommy. I was a writer!

Being a writer gives me a sense of purpose that being a mom does not. While in theory I know that I am molding the lives of my children, and helping them grow into responsible and (hopefully) law-abiding citizens, that is simply not enough to get me through the day-to-day. Writing allows me to use my brain in a way that, frankly, motherhood does not. In my writing, I can utilize an adult form of self-expression, even if I am writing about poop and sleep deprivation.

And while I don't get paid to broadcast my thoughts and feelings on the Internet, I still get immense satisfaction when I see that seventy-five of my Facebook friends took a gander at my blog after seeing that I wrote something new, or when an old friend says she loves reading my blog because it makes her laugh, while making her realize that her own parenting trials aren't so unusual. These moments of recognition are my payment, because knowing that I made someone laugh means more to me than any paycheck ever could. When you make someone laugh, it's validating: You know they are laughing because they have been there too, and that maybe your latest rant on how your kids are driving you crazy doesn't make you such a bad parent after all.

Tonight I'm at yet another cocktail party.

Another handsome stranger, this time standing at a safe and reasonable distance, asks me, "So what do you do?"

"I'm a writer," I say confidently.

"Oh you are?" he asks, clearly very interested in what I will say next. Surely he thinks I will tell him I write for the *New York Times* or *Vanity Fair.* That I write hard-hitting news stories about world hunger and unrest in the Middle East.

"Yes I am."

And I just leave it at that.

When not chasing after her endlessly energetic children, **Jennifer Van Santvoord** writes whenever she can. Mommy by day and writer by night, she publishes in various parenting blogs as well as her own personal blog, *milesfromperfect.com.* Jennifer lives in Marin County, California, with her husband and their three kids.

Become the Hero

Pamela Alma Weymouth

Above all, be the heroine of your life, not the victim.
—Nora Ephron

IF YOUR DADDY LEAVES YOU AT THE AGE OF THREE IN THE hands of a mother whose love is as predictable as the hurricanes in New Orleans, you make deals with yourself and your future children: You will have a TV family like the one on "Family Ties." Your future husband will toss off his lace-up, pointy-toed dress shoes and say as he swings through the front door, "Honey, I'm home!"

You interpret history: Your lanky, motorcycle-riding, striped-sock-artist daddy left because you were not cute enough, funny enough, good enough. Since your older sister stole the pretty-good-girl role (and your rightful breasts) you will become the funny bad-girl sidekick. Maybe if you make enough noise, your daddy might hear the sound of the ruckus you're causing, like that night you got blackout drunk just to show him that you needed him back, only he didn't read the subtext under your torn-up jeans and your muddy face. Instead he carried you straight past the blue-suited doorman guarding your Manhattan high-rise, delivering you straight back to your mother the way a Maoist might have delivered a neighbor up to the Red Guard for some reeducation.

If your lanky-legged mother tells you that your grand-daddy was the smartest and funniest man alive until he blew his brains out with a 28-gauge shotgun (before you were born and before she fell in love with your introverted-gypsy daddy) you learn early that humor is the flip side of tragedy. You decide to become as funny as your granddaddy because when your mummy is laughing, the roots of trees are allowed to remain in the earth; she touches your curls and says, "Isn't she clever?"

When you are ten you study your favorite Uncle Teddy, who can wiggle one ear while raising the opposite eyebrow. He pulls quarters out of his sleeve and plays old country songs about men in jail: two-timing cheaters who left their women broken-hearted in rundown motels on the way from here to nowhere. But when Teddy disappears into a mental hospital (because he's got a booze- and drug-related habit) you begin to believe that you will indeed lose every man you love.

You tuck your fury and grief into diaries, locked with golden keys or unlocked, tied up with leather ropes or pink silk ribbons. You have hundreds of them now, all your life sealed up in little books that are onyx, emerald, or blood-red, hand-painted or tie-dyed, decorated with butterflies, fairies or words like *Hope, Dream, Wish.*

One day, these handwritten letters begin arriving in the mail addressed to The Chief—which is you, because you've started your own newspaper, the *Monday News*—because like your mummy and your grandmama and your dead grand-daddy you want to be a journalist, a storyteller, a world-changer. You begin publishing Uncle Teddy's stories, "The Funny Farm

Follies," about the characters inside the mental hospital, who punch their pillows instead of their mothers, talk to their alter egos, cheek their meds or wear socks on their hands. After you've shared these stories with two hundred of your family friends, the East Coast literati that is (writers, politicos, artists), you see that your uncle is still the quirky story-spinner. Even locked up, he can slip through the bars of his confinement with a few well-chosen words, making your hardheaded mother laugh at something she was hollering about only yesterday. On visiting day, you bring Uncle Teddy a little lightbulb that you made in fourth-grade science. It's just a tiny bulb and one AA battery, but when you press the two wires together it lights up.

Because what you planned when you were five doesn't always turn out, you don't publish your first novel at twenty-one; you don't win a Pulitzer at twenty-five; you don't bring peace to the Middle East.

One day you wake up and you're forty-three. You're married to an underemployed stilt-walker, not the Jewish novelist with the cookie-baking mother. You have the requisite babies, you do the couples therapy, you hang in for long enough that you begin to think you've beat the family curse, until one day your toddlers are old enough to allow you to finish your tea before they throw themselves over the garden fence. You have cooked the requisite fish sticks and put your three-year-old twins to sleep (after they attempted to exit the cribs twelve times). You have nearly killed yourself twice today: once tripping over your husband's sneakers in the middle of the staircase and a second time when his *Alice in Wonderland* stage fork (that he insists on keeping at a precarious angle in the garage) nearly decapitated you and your sleeping son, as you exited the car (after you drove up and down every San Francisco hill, depleting enough ozone to compete with China, just to achieve the nap). You hammered in the rusty nails sticking out of the floor so that your boys would not stab themselves and now you (who were never taught the finer points of housekeeping) are scrubbing the floor to get the tomato stains off the cabinets. You have not written a word in sixty-six days and your husband is watching another TV autopsy show because he says *the dishes can wait, and by the way, did you notice that the bathroom sink is clogged?*

This is how, on the day you discover your first wrinkle, you find yourself divorced, in need of a date, slumped inside your dented red Honda in front of your falling-apart fixer-upper in a suburban outpost of the city of San Francisco, the city that used to be yours. The house that was supposed to harbor you (and save your sons' college fund) is now collapsing under the weight of the downpour. The Italian contractor, who promised to *take care of you baby,* has just quit after an argument with the Rat Man, who promised not only to remove the dead rats from the heating ducts but to remove the mold too (and only for ten grand) and only because you're a single mom, just like the woman who raised him. He was even so generous as to accompany you to the bank, where he stood watching your sons while you withdrew the cash.

You watch the rain tap dance its way through the roof, spreading the toxic mold that pushed you and your sons into a temporary rental on the side of the freeway, in a part of suburbia where the grass is cut to match the haircuts of the men who still have hair, and the bald men drive shiny cars to replace what they've lost, while the women on the playgrounds (who are not the brown-skinned nannies) look as if they have just been varnished and set to dry.

There are two empty toddler seats in the back, broken cheddar bunnies on the floor, the air stinks of sour milk, and you've got nowhere to go on a Friday night but back to an empty borrowed house. For the last five years you've read *Goodnight Moon* and sung your way through the Americana songbook, censoring the parts about the *dead and gone forever, dreadful sorry, Clementine,* as if you might, for a bit longer, be able to shield your children from the injustices of dead coal miners and the rest of the world's disappointments. You have said goodnight one by one to the stars, to the spoon, to your dead dog, to the crooked moon. Sure, it was a circus: food splashed across the walls, double tantrums, arguments with a man over why he couldn't do more—but it was your circus. On this night, your goodnight will be said through the telephone line to two four-year-olds who will cry, "I want you Mama, I want you."

Two days of loneliness stretch out in front of you like a hitchhiker's highway. You've got nowhere to go but back to the beige-ness of your temporary condo on the wrong side of the freeway, your only company an oversized television set offering up shows like "The Bachelorette" or "The Biggest Loser."

You stare at your cell phone trying to figure out who to call. Everyone on your list of "favorites" is married with children, which means they are changing diapers, running baths, cooking dinner, or having scheduled sex. Your single friends moved back to New York a long time ago, and now you know what your sister meant when she said of divorce what they say in AA: *You need to make new friends.* You wipe your nose on your sleeve, because unlike good mothers you have no tissues in your car.

Then you remember the story-slam contest and some instinctual will to swim to the surface thrusts you into gear. You accelerate toward your computer, north on Highway 101. The theme of the contest is "What went wrong?" which reminds you that one day this will be funny. Words and wit are the last thing you have that are still yours—the only thing the State of California cannot divide up fifty-fifty.

With thirty minutes until starting time, you throw a sparkly-blue sweater over your fitted blue jeans and your high-heeled, bad-girl boots. You dunk your face into a sinkful of scalding water. At stoplights you apply black eyeliner, silver eye shadow, poppy red lipstick.

Reciting your story as you drive: Vertigo-Mold-Contractor-Daddy all the way to the doors of the Mill Valley Library; you scratch your name onto a little piece of paper and throw it into a hat.

When they pick your name out of the hat your heart is beating hard and fast, as if you've just had it jump-started. Adrenaline propels you toward the podium, where you stand for a second taking in a room thick with books, history, and two hundred strangers. They are wearing Prada heels, Docksiders, and REI's latest hiking boots. An hour ago you were judging their cars, their politics, and the size of their freeways. Right now, you want them to love you and you'll do anything to get a laugh. You are not allowed to use notes, so you must pull the story from your head. You hold on tight to the microphone; the audience is silent, waiting.

You begin with the vertigo, the day after you fell out of your marital bed and the floor reached up to slam you in the face—the day after you talked to the divorce attorney, who charged you seven hundred dollars (for one-hour-fifteen) to tell you that you ought to be generous with your assets, that you'd be the one to support your ex even if he had incurred a financial and emotional debt that was larger than your capacity to forgive. Her fee becomes a lawyer joke, and once the audience begins to laugh, your pace picks up, your hands become animated, and the words begin to flow. You make fun of yourself because a flawed narrator is more three-dimensional, and once you've done this, you can make fun of their lawns and their Spandex biking gear because now they'll let you. The house collapse becomes a slapstick comedy, like a set of dominoes falling with the tap of a finger, or like the false Hollywood stage-fronts in *Blazing Saddles,* because when you fall in love with a man, you don't see the mold beneath the cabinets until you're already committed. The comment your daddy made about your problems being mild in comparison to the tsunami that hit Fukushima—this makes them roar. The clincher is that the divorced eco-oil mogul, the one the real-estate lady promised you, is actually stuck in Japan. As you exaggerate, alliterate and metaphor your way through, you begin to transform your story rather than being shaped by it. Your tragedies lead to epiphanies that maybe you didn't have back then, but they become true in the telling.

When it is over, strangers stand in line to shake your hand. The judges give you the winner's prize: a book of free coupons for library books. When a narrow-faced man in a leather jacket asks you out for a drink you smile and say, "No thanks," because this time you don't need saving, or care-taking, or anything at all.

Pamela Alma Weymouth has an MFA in creative writing from the University of San Francisco and writes a humor blog for the Huffington Post on parenting and divorce. Her writing has appeared in the *Marin Independent Journal* and several anthologies including *Best Women's Travel Writing 2009* and *Hot Flashes: Sexy Little Stories and Poems I & II.* She has received awards from *Glimmer Train* and *Traveler's Tales.* Pamela is currently at work on a book of essays, *Surviving Twinland: The First Six Years.*

Not Afraid of Words

Steven Friedman

A RIVER OF PROCRASTINATION FLOWS WITHIN ME, ALTER-
nately surging over the shore or ebbing quietly against the
banks of my soul.

*Just as I finished that sentence, I dashed over to ESPN.com to check on col-
lege football scores. Why do today what I can put off until tomorrow and the next
day and beyond?*

In the sixth grade, I had weeks to finish preparing for a social
studies debate on the merits of Athens versus Sparta. The weekend before the debate, I finally went to the library and filled a
few note cards with bullet points about Sparta. But the history
book I had been using, filled with information about brawny
Spartans and brainy Athenians, could've been about quantum
mechanics. It was difficult to understand and the topic didn't
interest me.

*As I completed that second paragraph I looked up to watch Miguel, my
nearly sixteen-year-old son, playing football on his PlayStation. Why do today
what I can put off until tomorrow and the next day and beyond?*

I was woefully unprepared on the day of the debate, my
stomach rumbling as I gazed out at my sixth-grade peers. I
hadn't actually read over my notes so I didn't know the material at all, and was clueless about how to debate. I hadn't paid
any attention in class or group work.

In the middle of the debate, as I walked up to the podium to present my case, my legs wobbly and my head aching, my voice halted as I opened my mouth. Someone yelled out to me and I said, "Huh?!?" which triggered a torrent of laughter.

I was mortified and metaphorically naked as my true self, lazy and irresponsible, shone through like a beacon on a fog-shrouded night before my classmates and teachers.

During the last three paragraphs, I broke away to text my fiancée in Colorado: "I know ways to pass the time" knowing that if Miguel sees this he'll roll his eyes.

In high school I waited to write essays for AP English until the night before, and only survived by using CliffsNotes. One time in college, during a year abroad in Israel, I started a ten-page paper on the modern history of Egypt less than 12 hours before it was due. The next morning I turned in the paper, written in longhand, replete with illustrations. The professor rejected it immediately.

I quit a job boxing up defective typewriters after one day. I quit another as an assistant janitor one summer after six hours.

Writing was to be my salvation. But writing is hard, often very hard, so it is not exactly the best domain for a chronic procrastinator. In college I wrote for the daily newspaper. One time I spent nine hours in the newsroom and finished an article at midnight just in time for the copy editors to review it, hours before it was to be typeset for the next day's paper.

Now I am working on a memoir, tentatively titled *It's Not About the Breasts,* which will chronicle in often painful detail our cancer journey from the time my late wife Verna was diagnosed with breast cancer in 2006 until her death in 2010. But I don't write very much. Well, I do blog. But, as one friend said,

"Blogging is like a one-night stand. Writing a book is like having a relationship. It requires hard work."

I work with elders full-time and am raising two kids. So my day ends at 9:00 p.m. and then I settle onto the sliding recliner, the computer perched atop my lap, and I read emails, check Facebook, play solitaire, and scan the day's news on various Web sites.

And instead of writing my memoir, I read memoirs by others. Or I read about writing. During Tracy Kidder's *Good Prose*, which featured excerpt after excerpt of really, really good prose from award-winning authors, I screamed to myself, "I will never write like this." And that sentiment bubbles forth almost every time I read a memoir or a nonfiction essay. My writing will never be as compelling or worthy because I am not compelling or worthy.

Why do today what I can put off until tomorrow and the next day and beyond? I just stopped writing to remind my son, who'd just finished his video game, to continue working on an essay due two days before Thanksgiving. He opened his computer but five minutes later, responding to a text from two friends, bolted outside to play football. Is procrastination contagious or genetic?

A month or so after Verna died I decided to join a writing group in order to motivate myself with regular assignments and feedback and interactions with my peers. The only one I found was a mothers' writing group sponsored by a local bookstore. Although it was all women, their mission fit mine: "We come together to share so we can write. We share our challenges, our worries, our successes. We share our words. We share the need for a push when things get tough."

I emailed the coordinator and, shockingly, she invited me to join the group. "We are looking for more men," she said. I'd love to say that joining made me renounce my procrastinating ways and forge towards the daily discipline of writing, writing, and writing. But that desire must come from within.

The bitter reality is that I am not always a procrastinator. I have trained diligently for and finished four Boston Marathons. This past summer the kids and I participated in a family bike tour in Colorado where we biked 152 miles over four cycling days, including a fifty-two-mile ride that featured scaling 10,660 feet over Vail Pass.

What I am is scared—scared of failure, scared of someone shouting out in the cafeteria and then laughing at my words, scared of not being good enough.

And what I have learned from my mothers' writing group is that everyone feels that fear—about writing, parenting, loving, working, just living. But we do soldier on as parents and lovers and employees. And as writers we bare our souls in front of hundreds (or gatherings of a few) about joy and pain and loss and celebration.

We write. I write. I write to conquer the demons of my past, the ones that held me back from achieving more in school and at work. I write because I can no longer put off today or tomorrow what I must now face: Life is too short and sometimes it shatters without warning. So I write to cleanse my soul and to shout, "I am here, please listen, I do have something to share."

Steven Friedman writes because he loves it, and also to keep his late wife Verna's memory alive for him and for his two children. Steven currently works with elders but has been a middle-school teacher, a car salesman, a drywall salesman, and a funeral director. He's always been a writer too, sometimes even getting paid. His first book, *Golden Memories of the San Francisco Bay Area,* was published in 2000. Verna once told Steven she'd be famous after she died, which just might be the case when he finishes his cancer journey memoir *It's Not About the Breasts.* Steven is in love again, but still misses Verna, his best friend and now his muse.

From Conception to the Empty Nest

*What to Expect When You're Expecting to Combine
Writing and Motherhood*

Lorrie Goldin

DO ASPIRING MOTHERS AND WRITERS EVER KNOW WHAT'S
coming? Probably not—if we did, the world would be signifi-
cantly emptied of children and books. Both our species and our
libraries depend on hopeful naïveté. Blind optimism is one of
nature's neatest tricks.

I initially was tricked into both the writing life and motherhood by an easy conception and labor. In college, I played
bridge every night until one o'clock in the morning, then ges-
tated my papers in the shower. Ideas, organizational structure,
and beautifully phrased paragraphs flowed as easily as the
water streaming down my back. Since word processing hadn't
yet been invented, I wasn't tempted to constantly revise, which
helped curb paralyzing perfectionism. I'd simply towel off and
transcribe my genius to the page.

Becoming a mother was just as easy. My first daughter was
conceived right after we discarded birth control. The pregnancy
was uneventful, and even labor didn't live up to its forbidding

reputation. Expecting to be doubled over in pain for about a day and a half, I wandered around Marine World the day Emma was born, experiencing the equivalent of mild menstrual cramps. I assumed it was the heat and the corn dogs. Right after we got home, my water broke, and Emma emerged less than two hours later—on Mother's Day, no less. It was the equivalent of assignments writing themselves after a night of bridge.

Ah, the seduction of beginner's luck! Maybe if I'd had to work harder at producing children or term papers, I'd be a better writer. Alas, my post-college writing "discipline" is patterned after my path to motherhood: Want it, fall into bed, and await results.

Sadly, desire and waiting proved insufficient for the tasks ahead. Just as children will not raise themselves, God will not choose you as his amanuensis. If you insist, as I most often do, on writing only when the spirit moves through you, you will discover that God, too, suffers from writer's block. Emma and planned C-sections notwithstanding, if you want to birth a baby or a bestseller, you can't escape the pangs of labor.

Welcome to reality and to the tedious isolation of being tied to an infant or a blank computer screen. At least babies seduce with their wriggly marshmallow bodies and toothless smiles, enticing you to stay with them by making you feel like the best mother in the world. The blank screen, on the other hand, destroys any notion of talent and just drives you away. Under the guise of "research," you forsake your botched creation, seeking comfort in endless Cutest Baby videos on YouTube. This continues until you suddenly realize you have your own cutest baby, and that you should have picked her up from daycare a half hour ago.

So while the maternal instinct is reinforced by coos and gurgles, or at least the threat of late fees, it's a lot harder to stoke the authorial instinct. In fact, it's more tempting and less consequential to be a negligent writer than a negligent mother. No one will call Child Protective Services if you stop feeding your creative impulse, or leave it alone for weeks at a time.

So why do it? Why write? For that matter, why have children? And seriously, why combine the two?

Because there's that urge. The uneasiness that sets in if your fingers haven't lingered on the keyboard for a while as your brain searches for just the right word. The longing for self-expression that begins as a tiny hollow in your gut you ignore until it mushrooms into full-body agitation to get your attention. You know you'd be better off taking up salsa dancing instead of staring at the blank screen while sipping your tenth cup of tea. But you just can't help yourself—the longing persists until it's fulfilled.

Wrestling with the urge to have children is similar. You tell yourself you can't afford it. Besides, how can you in good conscience bring a child into this calamitous world? You say how lucky you are to have the freedom to travel, then spend the day sobbing after passing a stroller in the park. So even though having kids will ruin your career, marriage, figure, and vacation plans, you ignore the evidence and trade in your identity to become a mother. You just can't help yourself—the longing persists until it's fulfilled.

Of course, not everyone feels the urge to write, just as not everyone wants to have children. But if the urge is there, and you ignore it or try to talk yourself out of it, it just gets worse.

It may seem crazy to combine motherhood with writing. But since mothers—expert multitaskers anyway—often talk themselves into having another baby by thinking, "Two can't be that much harder than one, at least they'll keep each other entertained," it's easy to see how it happens.

Besides, given the similarities and efficiencies of scale, why not do both? You're already living in your sweats all day anyway. Both roles are underappreciated and underpaid. They share that peculiar warping of time—never enough while simultaneously endless. Whether writing or mothering, often whole days will go by with nothing to show for it, not even dinner.

Even better, children supply material, and writing supplies you with a connection to the life you used to have, when you had clothes that fit and never introduced yourself as so-and-so's mother. And what better payback for the children who have stolen your identity than to appropriate theirs by writing about them?

So there you are in the middle of the night, with your baby and your journal, sleepless, irritable, consumed with buyer's remorse. You want to give it up, but you can't. Might as well accept that there's no going back, and that you'll never be free of self-doubt. Rest assured, however, that there are predictable, parallel stages to motherhood and writerhood.

Eventually you settle into some kind of routine. As a new mother you may be bored and isolated, but you're also intoxicated from imbibing every smile and spastic lurch, shocked and awed by the wonder of what you've created, and the terror of sticking with it no matter what.

This, along with the newfound ability to shower and leave the house, compels you to join a mothers group for mutual aid and comfort, swapping anecdotes and tips for making it through the hard stretches of self-doubt. It also leaves you secretly wondering how much the other mothers hate you because your baby is sleeping through the night; why only your libido is still AWOL; how come your baby's motor skills aren't advancing as nicely as those of the other babies; and whether or not you should share the name of your great babysitter. Still, you couldn't live without your fellow moms. At least it gets you out of the house.

Joining a mothers group is a precursor to joining a writing group when your baby (who has finally crawled!) becomes a toddler. Now you are ready to reclaim your identity beyond competing with other mothers in the developmental-milestone Olympics.

Under the guise of promoting father-baby bonding, or after promising your husband more sex, you escape the house monthly to join other writers for mutual aid and support. And to sneak a glass of wine. This group, too, saves your life, with its laughter, commiseration, and tips for surviving self-doubt. Also familiar are the secret fears about why your writing isn't advancing as nicely as others', or, if it is, how much everyone will hate you if your piece is accepted, and whether you must share the name of your editor. The only real difference is that by now you realize that stories of resurgent libidos are pure fiction.

But all in all, this is a delightful phase. Your baby is taking his or her first tentative steps, and so are you! It's a time full of magic, laughter, and low expectations. Seriously, you're the mother of a toddler, how can anyone hold you to deadlines? Plus, there's a large audience of other captive mothers who are besotted with your amusing scribblings about potty training. Indeed, potty training is a good metaphor for this phase of writing. You may be pretty hit-or-miss, but there's lots of enthusiasm over your every production.

Potty training also heralds the arrival of the terrible twos, a phase notorious for epic clashes of will, tantrums, and loud proclamations of "No!" Some of these battles occur with your child, but the real doozies are inside your head: Should I write while she naps? No! I should do the laundry. Or take a nap myself. Or have a gin and tonic. Just as the terrible twos are characterized by approach and avoidance, so is this stage of writing.

But since everything looks better after a nap or a gin and tonic, you carry on, happy with your modest scribblings and decorating the refrigerator door with your toddler's. Before you know it, it's time for preschool, another great phase. With a routine and a modicum of self-management, life hums along. Again, there are low expectations, with gold stars all around just for showing up. Your preschooler garners lavish praise for the ability to sit in a circle. And you are pretty proud of yourself for circling your computer and occasionally sitting in front of it between drop-off and pick-up.

This continues through the early primary grades, an exciting time of curiosity and mastery. You, like your eight-year-old, gain confidence in your abilities, and can even manage to work at your desk for more than twenty minutes without fidgeting or incessant bathroom breaks. You're bursting with pride at your own as well as your child's ability to fill the page with laboriously crafted words.

After about third grade, it becomes clear that being God's gift to the world counts for nothing. Those who push themselves beyond the specialness of mere existence start to pull away from those who don't. Your child is shocked to learn that despite his winning smile, he is lagging behind his peers academically. You remind him that if he wants better results, he needs to put in the effort and actually turn in his homework. He says he doesn't care, but you know he's lying, because that's what you tell yourself when you blow off a deadline. It doesn't escape you that if you followed your own advice, maybe you'd have more to show for your writing than the deep-down knowledge that you're a fraud.

Procrastination and tears and complaints of how unfair it all is (teachers, editors) gradually give way to the satisfaction of hard work and accomplishment. Voila! Your child's math homework earns a "Nice work!" and you get a form rejection letter with a handwritten postscript that says, "Keep trying!"

So you do, and you and your child advance to middle school. But beware the bully on the playground and especially the one in your head: the one who taunts you that you're full of shit and threatens to relieve you of your lunch money and self-esteem. Walk away, fight back, do whatever it takes to vanquish the bully. Remember, middle school doesn't last forever. It gets better. And so does your writing.

Around about now, you will also start to feel the sting of rejection. Your thirteen-year-old ignores your texts. Your submissions don't even generate an auto-reply. Get used to it. Try not to take it personally. This stage lasts for a really long time. But you will learn to tolerate it, and it, too, eventually gets better.

Adolescence brings not just rejection, but greater skills and higher stakes. Exuberance and swagger are coupled with excruciating self-consciousness. Your teenager will not leave the house with that zit on his forehead no matter what you say. "You don't understand!" he laments, certain you are clueless about what awaits him if he subjects himself to scrutiny. But you understand him all too well, because no matter how much your writing group begs you to submit your imperfect piece, you just can't.

And the mood-swings! Your daughter gets a callback for the lead in the school play, and you get a nibble on a query letter. All is bliss, until your daughter's best friend gets the part, your follow-up goes nowhere, and your friend's piece is published in a magazine that pays. After your daughter finishes ranting about how her friend is always sucking up to the drama teacher, you talk about how disappointment builds character, how proud you are that she congratulated her friend, and that she is neither a failure nor a bad friend for feeling envious. "It will be you next time," you say, because this is what your friend said to you. Meanwhile, you wonder why you're such a failure, if your friend slept with the editor, and whether she'd mind introducing you.

You're almost grown up by now, so you, like your teenager, suck it up and move on. Life is too busy for brooding, what with papers to write, college applications to complete, editors to seduce. You encourage your senior not to leave everything until the last minute, but you're both pulling all-nighters to meet your deadlines, praying that the server won't crash.

With luck and a case of Red Bull, you make it. Your kid gets into college and you get a provisional acceptance from a paying venue! But don't celebrate too hard—just as colleges withdraw their offers if seniors don't deliver in their final semester, so do editors. You're hung over, sick of it all, but it's back to the books—for final exams and another rewrite.

Ready or not, it's time to launch. Sending your baby out into the world brings an enormous rush of pride and accomplishment. And anxiety. What if your daughter's roommates don't like her, and your piece bombs? Neither one should ever have left home.

Your daughter's first semester is rough. She misses her friends. She cannot get started on the three term papers due next week, and won't ask her professors for guidance because she doesn't want to pester them. She's spending too much time on Facebook to see if her high school boyfriend changes his relationship status. As you soothe her through many sobbing phone calls, you remind her that professors love it when students come to office hours, and that it's too soon to consider transferring.

Meanwhile, your essay lamenting the empty nest has gotten published—to mixed reviews. Someone leaves a comment saying how lucky your child is to have escaped your neurotic clutches. Mostly your words fall into a black hole of no reaction beyond the obligatory kudos from your friends and family. Getting published has changed nothing, except that you are now one of those obnoxious people using Facebook only for self-promotion. You're about ready to burn all your journals and shut down your account until your writing group talks you down, reminding you that everyone promotes themselves on Facebook.

By spring your daughter is making better grades and better friends. She has a new boyfriend and has joined the environmental club. Things are looking up. They're looking up for you, too. With the kids gone, you've rediscovered why you married your husband in the first place. And since so many Facebook friends shared your piece, even your numbers of "likes" and hits are up.

But it's not really the numbers that count. It's the call you get from the child who not so long ago rejected your hugs and advice. After listening to her roommates' horror stories about their parents, she just wants to thank you for being a good mom. Or the email you get from a stranger, a gay dad, who somehow saw your post in support of marriage equality on an obscure blog months after it first appeared. "Thanks for your piece," he writes. "Maybe it'll shift a mind or two, if only an inch at a time."

That's how it is with writing and parenting. It's like putting a message in a bottle and casting it into the ocean, not knowing what will become of it, if anyone will ever notice or care about what you've launched with such hope and dread. Then one day, long after you've reconciled yourself to your message being lost forever at the bottom of the sea, you get a note from someone on a distant shore, saying how much your words mattered.

What an awesome responsibility and privilege it is to shift a mind or two, if only an inch at a time. It's why we send those words out into the world, or bring children into it.

But now what, now that they're launched? The clatter of kids no longer reverberates in your head all day. What's given you purpose and meaning and a house that looks like it barely survived Hurricane Katrina is gone. Disoriented, you wander into your daughter's room and marvel at how neat it is. You make a cup of tea, savoring it since it poses no scalding risk to babes in arms and will not be appropriated by your teenager as he dashes out the door calling, "Thanks, Mom, no time for breakfast!" There are no carpools to interrupt your day.

There are also no deadlines, now that your piece has been published. What's given you purpose and meaning and a house that could be featured on "Hoarders" is now gone. Disoriented, you start to clean up stacks of papers and dirty dishes.

You make another cup of tea, savoring it since it is only the second of the morning and not a measure of your procrastination. There are no conversations with editors to interrupt your day.

Ah, this is more like it, a well-deserved break! You could get used to this peace and quiet, with no demands. If only it didn't feel quite so . . . well, empty.

You feel a little tug—that urge again. Just as amnesia about pushing a melon-sized baby through a narrow passage lures many mothers into an encore performance, writer's amnesia does the same. Then it's labor and delivery all over again.

As crazy and exhausting and difficult as it is—mothering, or writing, or, God forbid, both—you can't imagine it any other way. It's not just the exhilaration of your baby's first smile, or seeing your name in print, or all the Hallmark moments that far outweigh the postcards from the edge. There's also the pride of accomplishment and responsibility, the joy of mattering, of leaving your mark.

But what truly transforms you into a mother, or a writer, is learning to bear with tedium and anxiety, to accept the ups and downs, to trust that something good will emerge if you persevere in your love and commitment. It may not be perfect. You could always have done better. But it's something you've shaped and nurtured from the spark of an idea to full-grown. A labor of love. Your creation.

Lorrie Goldin is a psychotherapist in private practice in the San Francisco Bay Area. Her personal essays, op-eds, and commentaries have appeared in the *New York Times* blog *The Motherlode* as well as *skirt! (skirt.com)*, *Underwired Magazine*, the *East Bay Monthly*, the *Sacramento Bee*, the *San Francisco Chronicle*, and the *Marin Independent Journal*.

She is also a regular contributor to KQED's "Perspectives" series. Lorrie blogs at shrinkrapped.com, and is at work on a book about ruptures in women's friendships. Married and the mother of two twenty-somethings, she has received a Participant Ribbon for every one of the events in the Developmental Milestone Olympics for both writing and mothering.

The Gingerdread Man

Mary Allison Tierney

REMEMBER LOOKING AT *NATIONAL GEOGRAPHIC* MAGAZINE portraits of jungle tribes? Lying on the living room floor, your head-bracing hand falling asleep, the scratchy carpet irritating the skin of your belly where your Hang Ten hand-me-down shirt had lifted up, turning the slick pages with your functioning hand. The smooth-skinned naked natives with their blackened nub smiles both fascinated and repulsed. The body manipulations: ritual tattooing, scarring, piercing, and stretching of the dark, jungle-moist skin was so other, alien.

I think about this as I seat myself at the dinner table on Christmas Eve, forcibly softening my squint of disapproval and holding my tongue in order to enjoy a rare visit from my eldest son.

Modestly pierced ears are pretty much ubiquitous at the table. My scientist brother-in-law has tiny hoops in each ear, but my eldest son has surgical steel in various gauges looping in and out in three different directions, plus rosewood bottle-cap-sized plugs in stretched lobes. But most festive is the thick, shiny, silver bull ring ending in double ball-bearings and dangling from his upturned nose—jewelry that would be more suited to a 350-pound Samoan, not my delicate-featured, freckled, blue-eyed Scots-Irish neo-primitive.

Plus, I think we can all agree that white-boy dreadlocks are unfortunate. Not just one, but two ambitious rope-heads are seated at our dinner table. Brothers—one dark, one red—eating only the quinoa salad. Seeing them seated next to each other, I recall rinsing playground sand and sweat from their toddler scalps as they battled with multiple Batman action figures—and me—in the tub. I would pour warm water from a *Toy Story* popcorn bucket as they covered their eyes with a washcloth, asking if I'm done almost as soon as the water hits their foreheads, the stream pulling their ringlets down their backs as the suds were rinsed away. Now those curls are matted and hidden in rough ropes that smell worse than they look and include beads, feathers, and remnants of camping on Mount Tamalpais.

The elder, the redhead, has crafted his signature look into a "dread mullet." He's cut the front short, grown a pompadour, bleached it, then shaved it down to a burr cut. With the red ropes pulled back, he almost passes as employable.

"The Gingerdread Man," as he calls himself, sits here before me six months into what we are collectively agreeing to agree is a gap year. He left college after his freshman year and he is the only person at the table who is happy about this. His freshman year of college was a busy one. He did well academically, but he also hopped freight trains, took up with a nefarious crew in Portland and earned an arrest record. He now uses the term "squat house" with casual familiarity and has four DIY tattoos. I'm gonna go out on a limb here and say he hasn't been wearing his retainer.

I'm enjoying Christmas Eve dinner with my family yet baffled by my poseur hobo. When he left school, he and his tribe went on food stamps because they didn't want to be tied down to summer jobs. He wanted to roam and since we, the evil fun-suppressors, wouldn't be sponsoring his plan, well, he showed us. He and I had a chat about integrity and I might have used the words "lacking a moral compass" when I forgot to use my inside voice.

Choosing a squat house in Oakland or the joint custody tribal van instead of his bed in our home. Opportunities rejected, intentionally festooned to appear unemployable, leaping headlong with gusto into risk-laden situations, all the while knowing he has options.

His reality is his choice.

My choice is to detach, enjoy my dinner, sip my wine, and breathe. I look at my kids and realize it was never my intention to raise houseplants, children who fear the world. I cannot control his twenty-year-old brain. I am fascinated and repulsed. I say nothing.

Mary Allison Tierney is a native Texan now living in the Bay Area and navigating a minefield of twenty-something, teenaged and perimenopausal hormones. She is a recovering private-school mother of two college-aged musician/artist-philosophers and a middle-school Whovian drummer with aspirations in fashion and science fiction. Her essays have been published in *The Sun* and the *Marin Independent Journal*. A novice surfer, a diligent trail runner, and encaustic painter (because melting beeswax with a propane torch is quite soothing), Mary Allison can also read metal-band logos and has on occasion been caught knitting.

The Heritage Doll

Paula Chapman

WHEN MY SON AIDAN WAS IN FIRST GRADE, HE BROUGHT
home a blue plastic "Friday Folder" at the end of each week.
Going through this folder together was our Friday afternoon
ritual. Aidan would eat a cheese stick or cookie while we sorted
through it. After mandatory expressions of enthusiasm over his
math prowess or writing improvement, most of it went into the
recycling bin, except the artwork, which mom guilt forced me
to add to a growing stack inside my office closet.

One week, a project in the Friday Folder caught my eye—
the Heritage Doll. Now, this was right up my alley since my
writing was inspired by stories from my family tree. At the time,
I was writing about Grandpa Louis' conscription into the German army in World War I and his subsequent efforts to come to
America. In contrast, his beloved sister who lived in America
at the time made the disastrous choice to return to Germany
amidst economic ruin.

I grew up with these family stories and, between the emotional pendulum swings of the death of my Grandma Lily and
the birth of my son in the previous few years, I felt the urge to
preserve them. My writing was a private refuge to deal with the
stresses of new parenthood, and I guarded my stories from family members until I was ready to share the final draft. Aidan and

my husband Shannon heard small bits and pieces over time, but not the full emotional content.

The instruction sheet for the Heritage Doll project detailed how to pick one line of family heritage and decorate the doll for class the following week. What to choose? My husband and I have similar roots, German and Swiss, so images of Bavarian *Lederhosen* and *Lodenhut* with pheasant feathers leapt to mind. Or perhaps a skier on the Matterhorn with a bar of chocolate in his hand and an exquisite timepiece on his wrist?

I held up the project sheets to Aidan and said, "This should be fun for us to do this weekend."

He grabbed a cookie out of the jar and shrugged. "Mom, I already finished it this afternoon."

Saddened, I flipped the page and saw the cutout doll we were to decorate.

Shaped like a gingerbread cookie, the doll fit snugly on the eight-by-ten-inch page. Within the curvy outline, the drawn-on details were black and white and the doll was wearing a basic T-shirt and shorts with a big smiley-face, like the yellow seventies buttons. That made me smile. Aidan might never be an artist but he had an eye for humor and fun. My eye wandered back up the page to the headband, and my first question was "Why is the doll wearing a headband?"

What the hell? was my second question. In the middle of the black headband was a white circle with an unmistakable, crooked black cross on it. I shook my head because that white circle couldn't possibly be what I thought it was. I brought the page up closely to my eyes as if it would change that despicable image. My mind tried desperately to come up with the reason why my sweet and sensitive six-year-old boy had drawn a Nazi swastika.

My heart seized as I slammed the pages down on the kitchen counter. No matter how I covered it, I could still see that awful image in my mind. With the story of my grandfather leaving his family behind in what was to become Nazi Germany, this symbol represented the type of tyranny he despised. I cringed, wondering what my grandfather would say of my son drawing this as entertainment. Had Aidan asked a teacher what a swastika was supposed to look like? Who had seen it? What did they think of our family?

"Aidan! Aidan! Get in here!" I shouted.

He ran into the kitchen, making the impatient face, where his brows pulled together and corners of his mouth pulled down. A very adult look on a very small face.

"What?" he said.

"Why did you draw this?" My tears were swelling up, and I couldn't keep the anxiety and hurt out of my voice.

Aidan took one look at my face and lost his cockiness, bursting into tears, "What? What did I do wrong? Isn't that the German flag?"

Speechless at first, I guided him over by the arm to the dining room table and we sat down, and then began to do something I never imagined I would have to do with my six-year-old child: explain the evils of Hitler and the Nazis and how some symbols have a tremendous amount of power.

"So we weren't Nazis?" he said, getting right to the point. His little adult-looking face belied the fact that he couldn't possibly understand all the implications of this question.

"No, honey, our family lived in Germany but we were not part of the Nazi Party," I said, my face still twisted from the emotion brought out by the conversation.

Finally, I asked the most important question.

"Why did you draw this, Aidan? Did you see something on TV, or did someone talk about it at school?" I held his hand, while probing as gently as I could, all the time wondering if he was mixing with extremist kids at recess.

"Mom, you're writing a story about Grandpa," he said. He brightened up as he ran out of the dining room and into my office. Waiting in the dining room, I searched my memory, wondering if I had ever made more than a cursory mention of the story. He returned with several books that had been stacked on the corner of my desk, including *The Rise and Fall of the Third Reich,* which I was reading to research the political and economic landscape in 1920s and 1930s Germany. There it was—a swastika on the book's black-and-white front cover.

"See, it is the German flag," he insisted.

Guilt flooded in. He'd put two and two together about my writing and our family, but unfortunately came up with the wrong answer because I had not taken the time to explain or thought he might not understand these things at six years old. Our conversations hinted at a young man going off to war and then a journey back across Russia by my grandfather and his two friends. Without my having given him any additional details, it was no wonder that, as a small boy, he listened and wondered what all of it meant. If he was like me as a child, he would be fascinated by these dark stories. I couldn't be angry and I shouldn't have been surprised.

"No, honey, it is not the German flag. Why don't we erase it and start all over again?" I said to a visibly relieved Aidan, who sighed deeply and ran off to get the big pink eraser. While he was out of the room this time, I noticed something else that I had missed in my initial glance at the Heritage Doll. In addition to the headband, the doll wore tennis shorts—white with two little crossed tennis rackets on them. Now I was even more confused. When did our ancestors turn into tennis-loving Nazis?

When he returned with the eraser, I asked, "Aidan, why is your doll wearing tennis shorts?"

Relieved to not be in trouble anymore, he regained some of his normal confidence. He rolled his eyes at me and said emphatically, "Because, Mom . . . Roger Federer. You know Roger Federer, the tennis player, right?"

My puzzled expression as I tried to connect the dots seemed to further exasperate him.

"He's Swiss. Remember, we're Swiss?"

Scary. This kid really did listen to me. Next time we talked about what I was writing, I would remember that.

Paula Chapman works in the investment-management field, but her writing is rooted in the years she was a journalism major at the University of Colorado. She has performed her pieces live at the Mama Monologues in Corte Madera and San Francisco's Lit Crawl. In 2013 Paula left sunny California for Minnesota with her husband, son and two English bulldogs, and is learning to love snow all over again.

Writing in the Pauses

Susan Knecht

ON A DIAGONAL HORIZON LINE BELOW, I COULD SEE THE Chrysler Building as we began our descent. The airplane landed us intact on the tarmac but the stroller was badly broken. For all of his three years my son knew something was different about this trip: while Mama attended her writers' conference, he and his dad would be visiting the Museum of Natural History and a big playground in a place called Central Park. Why couldn't Mama come along? She was writing her book. She was always writing her book.

I sneezed into my hundredth tissue. In hindsight I realize that the multicolored congestion was probably swine flu, but I would not have missed the Pitch-and-Shop conference. It was billed as *the* conference to learn how to craft your pitch and then sell your novel idea to editors of the big publishing houses. With my Kleenex and Z-Pak of azithromycin, I had become a soldier for art. I blew my nose hard. It was New York, and somehow—unbelievably—a whole decade had passed since I had been home.

The limousine pulled up to the curb at the arrivals terminal.

"Clinton Avenue," I said to the driver. My head spun as we made a left onto the teeming street at the foot of the Williamsburg Bridge; bikers and pedestrians descended from Brooklyn like racers while motorists fought for the right-of-way. Our tenement building was situated just next to a hair-braiding salon and cell phone repair shop. The old was conflated with the new: I was brought back to my NYU days of writing and dreaming of getting published.

How wonderful: my son unpacking Cozy Bear, his doll Naima, and a large unnamed teddy he had hastily stuffed into his small suitcase that morning. He was to sleep in the only bedroom of our first-floor walk up. No matter that it was a vacation rental for a long weekend, he took to heart what the owner Fausto, a doting Brazilian man, had said: "I do my art here, my wife her photography. It's a perfect space for your boy." And it was. My son toured the three main rooms with me trailing; through the living room windows the twinkling skyline of the Lower East Side reflected in his eyes.

The bedroom was the real draw for my son. Impossibly, it overlooked a backyard: beyond a rarity for New York and certainly for the Lower East Side. It was early spring and still too wintry to explore the overgrown twigs and bramble surrounding a square of concrete patio. So he made do with the apartment's various curiosities: the two bathrooms, one with a toilet and a shower and one with a tub and a shower that sprayed the whole floor with a fire hose's intensity; the tiny, postage-stamp-sized kitchen that later would barely store our leftovers from the tapas restaurant. My son explained why the animals needed to be where he placed them on his bed as he unpacked shirts, his softest dinosaur pajamas, and a disproportionate number of library books.

My husband and I would sleep on a pullout futon in the crowded living room just under the bay windows. That night while Rowan played in the bath with his dad, I wrote my novel pitch on that bed. New York, the city, the rhythmic beat had always been synonymous with writing and it was again this night as one of my protagonists, Lila Lesser, returned after the War in 1945 with her baby granddaughter Isabel to the Jewish Quarter in Venice, haunted by a terrible memory of the family that is lost to her. The words flowed as they hadn't in some time and I was grateful to the city muse and the car horns honking on Delancey Street.

The next morning I headed uptown: the conference was held at a midtown hotel. At the subway entrance in SoHo, Rowan grabbed a strand of my hair when I bent down to hug him; my husband winked. While I pitched my novel to editors, they visited the Maclaren Store where they were happily received and the broken stroller was fixed on the spot. The irony of it, I would think later: that a place once overrun in the eighties with junkies and artists barely scraping by was now home to yuppie retailers, the art movement having been subdued, farmed out to Brooklyn; how impossibly surreal to be here amongst all of that, a mother of a son, with a novel still gestating.

The writer part had always been clear but the mother part murky like the duck pond in Central Park years ago, cigarette butts floating on top like breadcrumbs for birds. I walked with purpose to my conference; my shoes were luxuriously comfortable. This betrayed my age: how many streets off Washington Square had I limped along in pointy Trash 'n Vaudeville boots trying to imagine Bob Dylan doing the same on Bleecker twenty years earlier? Barely nineteen years old. A whiff of clove cigarettes evoked high school in Long Island mixed with freshman year and the briny river air outside the revolving doors of

Bobst Library; the slim volume, Andre Gide, on my lap on the Long Island Railroad train back home.

Later that evening reunited with my family, my pitch successfully accepted by three editors, two of whom had asked to see the first chapter and one the full novel, I half expected to see the *hamantaschen* of my youth in the bakery window on Ludlow Street, but rows of mini cupcakes iced in Hello Kitty pink greeted me instead. It was auspicious as far as beginnings go and we smiled a lot, my husband and I, owning the sidewalk for that minute.

"Can I have one?" My son's mouth was poised an inch from the window; he pointed to the cupcake's pink icing. I smiled, wanting so much to give him that and more. It was New York that made me think this, I was sure, the city with its promise to write and write well, be known and respected by other writers. The conference had sparked an old longing that was closer this time to fruition, I thought. I wiped some icing from my son's mouth. It was sweet like this day and pink as the sunset over the Hudson.

Susan Knecht spent her childhood in Brooklyn, Queens, and Long Island. Currently a psychotherapist in private practice in San Francisco and Menlo Park, she attended New York University and graduated with a bachelor's degree in English literature from Bates College, where she was the editor of the literary magazine, *The Garnet*. She has written poetry, plays, short stories, and narrative nonfiction. Susan is currently at work on the fourth revision of her novel *The Drowning Party*.

The Reluctant Author

Claire Hennessy

AS MY MASSEUSE, DIANE, PUMMELED A PARTICULARLY painful knot in my wobbly left buttock, she paused suddenly, her hands pressing into my butt cheek, and then announced:

"Claire, you *have* to start writing!"

"What?" I muttered, teeth clenching in pain.

"You need to write!" she declared again. "The spirits are telling me. You have to start writing."

Diane, or Di as she prefers to be called, is someone to whom the spirit world makes fairly regular contact. She is a sports massage therapist and Reiki master and once a month or so I visit her at her lovely house overlooking farmland, less than a mile from one of the best beaches in Sussex on the south coast of England. Because she knows I have strong spiritual beliefs and an open mind, and because she knows I won't immediately call the funny farm to have her hauled away, she feels comfortable passing on messages from various spirits who come to call. I normally try to go with the flow but this one had me flummoxed.

"I thought that's what you said, but why on earth would I do that?" I asked.

"I don't know, but they are insisting you start writing," she said with a shrug.

My mind was distracted from our weird conversation at this point by Di's attacking my right buttock as though it were a hunk of barbecue meat that needed hammering flat.

The next few times I saw Di she continued to mention that the spirits wanted me to write, and I kept refusing and so we went on, in a spiraling circle of strange conversations that I was glad my mother didn't overhear, as I knew exactly what she would say and it would involve men in white coats carrying straitjackets. Eventually, I demanded to know what these interfering, annoying spirits wanted me to write about. Di looked at me, exasperated.

"Honestly, Claire, how about this life-changing event that is happening to you right now?"

A single mum of two kids, living in rural England, I had recently reconnected with my very first boyfriend, "Bug," from when I was a mere thirteen-year-old schoolgirl. I had not set eyes on him since I had unceremoniously dumped him over thirty years ago at boarding school. But a bit tipsy coming back from the pub late one Friday night, I had found Bug on a school reunion Web site and rashly emailed him, not thinking it would develop into anything, as he was living on the opposite side of the world in California. Much to my surprise, a few tentative early emails had ignited a passionate rekindling of the old flames. After a few months of intensive communication via email and Skype, we nervously met to see if the chemistry was still there. Much to my surprise, we were still smokin' hot. We made quite a few trips back and forth across the Atlantic and even introduced our families, including the kids, with mixed success, especially where Bug's daughter was concerned. Blinded by our love, we plowed on regardless, unable to stop what we had restarted. Friends had been saying our unusual and highly romantic love story would make a great film, but I had not for one moment considered writing about it. I only wrote emails these days, plus the odd letter to my grandmother.

Besides, didn't you need some sort of training to write?

Even though I had never thought about writing, I'd always been a reader. I started very young with the bestselling books by English author Enid Blyton, and hadn't stopped since. If I don't have at least three books waiting in the to-be-read pile I start to worry. Reading is my escape, my means of calming down if I am angry or upset; it's a way to unwind and forget the stinky piles of dirty laundry, the grisly gift of mouse entrails from the cats or the guilty stack of unpaid bills.

Di, however, was like a dog with a bone and wouldn't let up. She would apologize, but said she couldn't help badgering me because the spirits wouldn't leave her alone. Finally, I'd had enough.

"Oh alright! I give up. I'll write. Just stop pestering me about it."

As soon as I agreed, Di stopped hounding me. It was weird to be hassled by a bunch of non-physical beings, but once the idea to write had been firmly planted in my subconscious, it was hard to uproot.

It was an intimidating idea, however, and it took me a couple of years to put pen to paper. It was especially easy to put off when my sizzling, long-distance romance had rapidly developed into something much more and we decided to get married. After an inordinate amount of drama and paper-work, the US immigration department finally decided I wasn't about to strap six tons of explosive around my ever-burgeoning middle and blow myself up on the Golden Gate Bridge, and we were given the go-ahead to live in America.

But then I found myself in the middle of the biggest upheaval of my life—moving lock, stock and barrel away from all my family and friends to an unknown future on foreign soil, dragging both my kids kicking and screaming along with me.

One of the agreements my new husband and I had made for me to give up my life in England was that I would not work for a while. I had had a varied career, from design and advertising, to an environmental charity, to exhibition trailer manufacturing. I had run my own corporate-events company organizing spy treasure hunts in Central London, and even worked on Internet radio stations. The past few years as a single working mother had been financially difficult, however, and my ex had not helped out much with child support, leaving me with a mountain of debt, which I told myself had nothing whatsoever to do with the massive stack of CDs which I was obsessed with buying and all the raucous evenings out with friends. I eventually paid most of it off when I sold my house in the picturesque seaside village in West Sussex on the south coast of England. I just wanted some time and space, not only to settle us all into our new home, but also so I could explore what I really wanted to do, something I could be passionate about, that would make my heart sing. I had always been so busy working and bringing up children, and rushing around seeing family and friends that I had never given myself a moment to think about where I was actually going with my life. What did Claire want to do? What was Claire really good at? What did Claire enjoy? Who was Claire?

And to be honest, I fancied being a kept woman for a while.

However, life at home in a brand new country was not all the fun and frolics I had naively anticipated. It was wonderful to wake up beside Bug every morning at last, but family life was also exhausting, confusing, and extremely stressful. Technically Bug and I were still in the honeymoon phase, but the first few months were brutal. We spoke the same language, but we said different things. We had different lifestyles, different values and different views on parenting. I realize now that blending families is a delicate art, requiring careful handling of all the different personalities involved. I came at it like a bull in a china shop, with no finesse and little sensitivity. Imagining myself to be fun and likable (because all my friends liked me, didn't they?) I rammed everyone together like an easy-mix sponge cake and expected a delicious masterpiece to emerge from the oven. Instead, the resulting mixture was lumpy, sour and, at times, even poisonous.

My husband's fifteen-year-old daughter was hostile to me from the moment she found out that I wasn't just one of her father's old school buddies, but his girlfriend. After we got engaged and I arrived in California with my kids and tried to instill some order into a household that had had very few rules, she fought me at every turn. She often wouldn't go to school, left a mess all over the house, and refused to wash up the dirty dishes after her mammoth baking sessions. My control-freak tendencies were honed to new peaks of dysfunction as I unsuccessfully tried to take charge of the chaos.

The night before we got married (admittedly only a month after moving in together), she shut herself in her room all day, only to emerge just before my husband left to spend the night at his best friend's house.

"Where are you going?" she demanded.

"I'm leaving for the night," Bug replied.

"What? Are you leaving me here with *her?*" She shot me a deadly look. "I hate her!"

Mark reprimanded her: "Don't be so rude. Apologize to Claire."

"No, I won't. I do hate her and I hate you. I don't want to stay here with her and I don't want you to get married!" she shouted at us both and then stormed back into her bedroom and slammed the door.

In hindsight, this should have given us an inkling of the jealous rages to come and it might have been wise to have addressed her concerns there and then, but at the time it seemed easier to leave her alone. Denial is a wonderful thing.

As you can imagine, that made for a delightful atmosphere at our small, intimate wedding ceremony. My stomach churned as I nervously read out my handwritten vows to my new husband. When I got to the part about loving his children as if they were my own, I didn't dare look at my stepdaughter-to-be, imagining her to have Medusa-like abilities, but even so I could still feel her sullen, angry stare burning hate-holes into me from across the room. I have never been more relieved to get away than when we jumped on the plane to our honeymoon in Hawaii, leaving the kids in the capable and compassionate hands of my Buddhist nun sister.

The upside of the challenges of my newly blended family was that they gave me plenty to write about. Feeling helpless and frustrated, I would write long emails that would never get sent. Somehow, the very act of writing down the stuff that was upsetting me helped, like the relief after bursting a pus-filled blister. But I knew that I wanted to write more. I wanted to see if I could tell the story of how Bug and I had first met and then reunited. I procrastinated, but eventually I could no longer ignore the little voices in my head telling me to write my book. Had I been infiltrated by aliens during Di's massages? Was I becoming schizophrenic? Would the Funny Farm men come to take me away? I wasn't sure; I just knew I had to write. I just didn't know how to start.

It was during this time that a new friend took me to a local mothers' writing group. I was hooked by these witty and intelligent women who made me laugh out loud one moment and cry the next, who shocked me with their sexually explicit references and scattered the word "fuck" about like it was confetti. I was relieved to know that I was completely wrong in my stereotypical belief that all Californian moms were uptight, politically correct and completely lacking a sense of humor. I immediately decided to join them.

At first I was daunted by the diverse talent in my writing group, but soon I came to realize that being mothers gave us all a common denominator—a way to connect. There's nothing that bonds complete strangers to one another quite like the horrific, shared experience of squeezing a camel through the eye of a needle.

I felt nervous and unsure of myself, but they told me to just start. It doesn't matter what you write, they said, the important thing is to write. You can improve and edit as you go along, but you have to begin somewhere. And so I did just that.

I was given a rickety, secondhand desk by a friend, which I managed to squeeze in next to my bed. I placed my new laptop on it with pride. I had been worried that when I first started writing I would find it boring and isolating, tapping away on the keyboard, sitting in my bedroom all by myself. But writing wasn't lonely at all. My desk overlooked our beautiful and sunny back garden; my beloved cats curled up on the bed and our dog sat at my feet.

Each month as my writing group came together to listen to speakers and workshop our pieces, I gained confidence and momentum. The other members were very flattering about my writing, saying they "could hear [my] voice" in my work. I thought they were just referring to my English accent, which had been my one overriding and continual success since landing on foreign soil. I had no idea that my British accent would be quite so coveted. Everywhere I went, people would stop me and ask what part of Australia I was from. Despite the antipodean slur, it was heady stuff.

As I grew more comfortable writing and publishing my lighter, more humorous pieces, I began to tackle harder issues. I started to dig deeper, be more honest, open myself up and let myself be vulnerable. I focused some of my attention on the difficult relationship with my stepdaughter. Writing about how I was failing as a stepmother helped me to accept that I was not perfect. I had made mistakes, plenty of them. But I was learning and trying not to repeat past behavior. I was gaining some self-confidence and delving deeper into myself. Writing even helped me to realize how much of a control freak I could be at times. And how trying to help other people was actually interfering, unless they had specifically asked for my help. (Surprisingly, nine times out of ten they hadn't.) I also talked too much, way too much. Not that this was a complete revelation, but when a wise friend shared the acronym WAIT—Why Am I Talking—I knew that it was meant for me.

Using the stresses and strains of my everyday life as topics to write about was not only enlightening me about my own hangups, but enabled me to express my feelings in the safe, supportive environment of my writing group. Learning to accept negative feedback and constructive criticism helped the quality of my writing and gave me the confidence to complete the first draft of my book. And now, when I'm holed up in my bedroom for hours on end, ignoring my family, the house is in a mess and I'm not helping with dinner, I always have the perfect excuse.

"The spirits are making me do it!"

British-born **Claire Hennessy** is writing a humorous memoir about reuniting with her childhood sweetheart after a thirty-year separation. Her work has appeared in the *Marin Independent Journal*, the charity fundraising anthology *Campaigner Challenges 2011* and on her personal blog, *Crazy California Claire*. She was awarded the Scribd Favorite Funny Story award for her essay "Valentine Surprise" and has performed her work alongside Anne Lamott, Kelly Corrigan and Ayelet Waldman. Claire is a founding member and Web-site editor of the Write On Mamas.

A Label She Loves

Dorothy O'Donnell

BY THE TIME MY DAUGHTER SADIE WAS IN FIFTH GRADE, I'd stopped asking the usual mom questions—*What did you learn today? How'd you do on your spelling test?*—when I picked her up after school. I had more important things on my mind. Like how people responded to whatever ensemble she'd painstakingly put together that morning.

"Did you get compliments on your outfit, honey?" I asked one spring afternoon as she slid into the back seat of my Subaru.

"Yeah," she chirped, her dark eyes dancing in the rearview mirror. "A lot of people really liked it!"

I smiled back. She had on a once plain, oversized lilac sweater from The Gap that used to be mine. It was headed for Goodwill until she rescued it from the donation bag I stash in the garage. Inspired by a shirt she saw on a TV show, she used a red Sharpie to adorn it with a pair of giant Angelina Jolie lips, transforming it from boring basic to hip fashion statement. The sweater was cinched with a wide, stretchy fuchsia belt. She paired it with grey jeggings tucked into last year's Old Navy motorcycle boots—boots I would have snatched up in a heartbeat if they came in my size. A pink-and-blue plaid fedora, tilted at a sassy angle across her forehead, completed the look.

She is fond of hats. Printed scarves. And for a touch of bling, her prescription glasses with the diamond-studded, purple frames. Anything that helps her stand out in a good way at school—a place where she's used to getting noticed for all the wrong reasons.

Sadie was diagnosed with a mood disorder and ADHD (attention deficit hyperactivity disorder) just before she turned six. As a result of treatment, the differences between her and her peers aren't as obvious today. She doesn't pop up from her seat every five minutes to march around the classroom or sharpen her pencil for the tenth time. She raises her hand (usually) instead of blurting out off-topic, sometimes nonsensical remarks. She doesn't erupt if a classmate accidentally brushes against her chair. She is better at following directions.

Yet traces of the reputation she forged back in kindergarten and first grade linger. Some kids still think of her as the bad girl. The girl who never listens. The weird girl.

Though she's smart, keeping up with her work is a struggle, even with extra support at school and help from a tutor. Problems with organization, focusing and processing information slow her down. She is all too aware that it takes her at least twice as long as most of her classmates to finish her assignments. That they can breeze through five pages of a book in the time it takes her to slog through one. That she'll never whip through fifty multiplication problems on a timed quiz fast enough to earn a coveted spot in the Math Champs Club.

Sadie's exclusion from such academic achievement "clubs" used to bother me just as much—maybe more. Like any mother, I want my child to have a chance to shine. I was a straight-A student for most of my school years. So was my husband. It was hard, at first, to accept that our daughter wouldn't naturally follow in our footsteps.

Eventually, I let go of worrying about her grades and whether she'll get into a good college. I try to focus on nurturing her many strengths instead. Especially her abundant creativity. The more she taps into it, the better her odds of finding her own path to happiness and success. I catch glimpses of this happening when she sings in chorus; writes a compelling— if poorly punctuated—story about her imaginary adventures on Rat Rock Island; or draws one of her trademark vividly colored, saucer-eyed fairies. And, increasingly, as she experiments with expressing herself through clothing.

There's no doubt the compliments she receives for her stylish getups have boosted her self-esteem. She may never look forward to school. But entering her classroom with a head-turning outfit each morning makes it a little easier.

Of course, living with a budding fashionista has its downsides, too. Sadie's refusal to venture out of the house in anything less than the perfect outfit often leaves her room looking as if it was invaded by a hoarder. Piles of rejected pants, dresses and shoes litter the floor and bed. Tops, sweaters and socks that failed to make the cut explode from her dresser. Her obsession has also made us late to school more than once. But when she feels good about what she's wearing, there's a swagger to her step as she struts to the car that makes such inconveniences a small price to pay.

As she prepares to enter middle school, Sadie is cultivating a new reputation, one I hope will buoy her as she navigates territory that can be tricky for any tween. She's becoming known as the girl with the cool clothes. The creative girl. The girl with style. And those are labels she wears with almost as much pride as her favorite boots and purple glasses.

Dorothy O'Donnell is a freelance writer whose work has been featured on Greatschools.org, Mothering.com, NPR and *Brain, Mother* (*Brain, Child* magazine's blog). She is an alumna of the Squaw Valley Community of Writers and is writing a memoir about raising a daughter with a mental disorder. Dorothy finds that writing has become a way for her to connect with others who are dealing with similar situations and to help erase some of the stigma associated with mental illness and disorders such as ADHD.

Of Rats and Deadlines

Laurel Hilton

IT'S THREE O'CLOCK ON THURSDAY AFTERNOON AND I'VE managed to avoid moving a story from my head to paper, yet again. This time, however, it has royally fucked up my day. My seven-year-old daughter Ellie has two pet rats, Teddy and Deacon. In a stroke of genius, I tell her that she can let them loose for some exercise in my office, while I furiously type a story that is due to be read in front of an audience at six this evening. Bad idea.

We keep the office door closed and let them scamper about for twenty minutes. Then just as I let Ellie know that it is time to collect the rats and scoop them back to their cage, my younger daughter, Luciana, pops open my office door. Damn. I hold Teddy in my hands, but where is Deacon? Not yet convinced he escaped into the environs of our entire house, we slam the office door shut and furiously tear up the room looking for him. After an hour of searching the office and then the rest of the house, still no Deacon. It is now 4:00 p.m. and with three-fourths of my story still to pour out onto the page, I couldn't care less if I ever lay eyes on Deacon's sleek, fawn-colored fur ever again. Ellie retreats to her room, grief stricken over her missing pet. I begin to write . . .

*Not even fifty years ago, Fullerton, in Southern California, where
I grew up, included vast stretches of orchards and farmland including*

crops yielding avocados, all kinds of berries, citrus and wheat. The very housing tract where my parents' house stands was an ocean of goldenrod flowers as far as the eye could see. Livestock was abundant and varied. Horses, cows, chickens, even ostriches came from Fullerton. (From the ostriches came a famous legend and the book Ostrich Eggs for Breakfast.*) My family owned two cows with my dad's business partner. One of them, Maisy, went on the lam when I was about five years old. She evaded the local police for three days before she met a tragic fate.*

There was iron livestock too; oil derricks dotted the landscape, bringing forth with their mighty pistons a decent amount of oil, I guess, because they're still there nodding their enormous steel heads more than forty years later. It seems like a cow town, but it wasn't, not really. It was actually quite a city even then, with plans in process for an airport, downtown civic area and possible super mall. I call it "ruburbal"— caught between receding farmland, quickly developing businesses and known as a bedroom community to Los Angeles just forty miles away.

I hear what sounds like a chuffing, scratching noise coming from my bookcase across the room. Pushing my chair back, I click "save" and amble over to see if the vigilante rat has installed himself behind my copy of *The Omnivore's Dilemma.* How fitting if that would be where I found him. After slowly sliding out the book, I find nothing but a few dust bunnies, not enough to make up one large, charming rodent. Back to the computer . . .

When I visit Fullerton a few times a year, I always walk the neighborhoods at night after the day has cooled and my kids are tucked in bed. I love this time of reflection and nostalgia, just me deep in my thoughts. I can close my eyes, breathe in deeply and recall the heady scent of citrus blossoms from my childhood. They've been replaced now by maturing palm trees and manicured lawns. One evening a woman walks nimbly not too far in front of me. From behind, she seems to be in her early sixties, with a trim figure and rolling pace. She carries a walking stick. My dog and I soon overtake her and make a wide arc to pass, but just as we do, she sees us and comments on my handsome cattle dog. (Well, he is.) As we face each other, I realize that she is closer to my parents' age of seventy. We start a random conversation of small talk and do not break stride, but quickly it turns to rapid-fire questions from the woman, who shows a keen interest in knowing how I landed in her neighborhood. Her neighborhood!

Another woman appears as if out of thin air. Where the hell did she come from? So, she's friends with Lady Number One. They have names, it turns out. Colleen and Lydia. I inform them that I grew up here, just one street over. They can't believe that, as we've never met, and they've both lived here for forty-five years. "It's true," I say to defend myself, and give them my parents' address, and rattle off the names of all our neighbors. They're impressed. They know the neighbors on either side of my mom. I mention my kids. Colleen's eyes narrow. "How old are you?" she quips. I'm shocked. I didn't think ladies of her age asked ladies of my age our age. "I'm forty-two," I say, a little surprised. "How old are you?"

Oh no, now I'm the instigator.

"Um, I mean, maybe you know my mom, seems like you would?" I say meekly. It goes on and on and now I realize it is some sort of strange generational pissing match. After running through every person that any of the three of us knows in a five-mile radius, we turn to tall tales, legends that get told from neighbor to neighbor over decades. "Well," says Lydia, looking at me. "You know that Frank Sinatra attended Laura Lasorda's wedding at your neighbor's house in the late eighties. I was right there and saw him get out of the limo."

"Oh yeah," I say breezily, as if this happened every day. "He was friends with the bride's father." I feel a little smug now.

Then, suddenly, I launch into a gripping retelling of how Maisy escaped from my dad's business partner's house in 1976 and ran around town for three days before the police found her. She was scared and bug-eyed, had a heart attack and died on the spot. My dad and his buddy had her butchered. We packed Maisy in our freezer and enjoyed tender-yet-anxious beef for many months. Colleen and Lydia are aghast at this story. So am I, frankly.

But then Lydia trumps me. "Our homes were built ten years before yours and I remember goldenrod and orange groves all the way down the hill. When the contractors came to grade your street, surge upon surge of field mice and spiders fled their destroyed habitat and infiltrated the foundations of our homes. It was awful," she says.

The septuagenarians have me beat with that one.

"Yikes," is all I can muster as a response.

The sky has deepened to a purplish blue hue matching the color of my bruised ego. This seems a good stopping point.

We bid our farewells and I wonder all the way back to my parents' house, what the hell has just happened and how many elder citizens in my old hometown have I enraged?

The next day, after returning from my afternoon jog, my mom approaches me, a bit confused.

"What happened last night, when you went out for a walk?" she asks. "Did you meet anyone?"

Oh boy, I did piss them off.

"Why?" I counter.

"Well, two ladies, Lydia and Colleen, stopped by looking for you today. They wanted to know if you were here and could join them for a walk. They seemed genuinely sad when I said you were out."

Ahhhh. I see. I guess I passed the test.
I was just asked for a senior play date.

With the last keystroke, I edit, save and hit print. The presentation is in twenty-five minutes. Deacon is still M.I.A. I don't care if that rat chews every wire behind my computer or eats through my entire book collection, I'm just relieved that I've made my deadline yet again. I grab my finished piece from the printer and cross the room to collect my bag, phone and a smoothie for the road. As I stride confidently to my office door, I hear another scraping noise and see the basket of clean laundry move suspiciously. When I pull Ellie's jacket from the pile, there is Deacon nestled in the hood. I call out cheerfully to Ellie that her beloved buddy has been found. As she scoops him lovingly to her shoulder, I swear I see a wink from his beady little eye.

Laurel Hilton is an eco-traveler and journalist. Her work is inspired by literary legends such as Paul Theroux, Martha Gelhorn, and George Saunders. She is currently working on a long-form piece on the impact of hydraulic fracturing on small towns in the western United States. Laurel was a finalist for the 2013 Notes & Words essay contest, and her essay "Freedom at the End of a Gun" will appear in *A Band of Women's* second anthology. She has contributed to KQED's "Perspectives" and performed at the Mama Monologues. She is the president of the Write On Mamas and resides in Mill Valley, California, with her husband, two daughters, a very loyal Australian cattle dog, and a couple of rats.

Two Mermaids

Beth Touchette

MY YOUNGER SISTER SUSIE AND I USED TO SIT ON THE smooth granite rocks by the Saint Lawrence River, shake our long, sun-damaged hair, and sing. We wore bikini tops and tied green beach towels around our waists to create fish tails. Our idea of what a mermaid looked like came from the image on the can of Chicken of the Sea tuna. The character had flowing blonde hair and a long mermaid tail, and her breasts were hidden demurely under her body's fish scales, unlike the breasts of most mermaids, which are human in form but hidden by falling hair, a strategically placed arm, or a well-positioned seashell. As the afternoon warmed, Susie and I occasionally dove into the fifty-degree water. We created mermaid tails by holding our legs together as we swam. Struggling to keep our heads above water, we always remembered to smile.

When I was eight and Susie was seven, we applied to be Weeki Wachee mermaids in Florida. These lucky women dressed in brightly colored bikini tops and fish tails, and swam in an underwater theater. They occasionally breathed through long plastic breathing tubes hidden in the scenery. I learned of the job opening from a tiny ad in the back of my Archie comic book. "We can be mermaids our whole lives!" Susie and I squealed as we filled out applications with our best cursive, which included i's dotted with hearts.

We never heard back from Weeki Wachee human resources. We knew that we were probably too young but we planned to apply yearly until we were accepted. When our mother said that she would never drive us to Florida for an interview we were crushed. She told us that it would be mostly drunk middle-aged men watching us perform.

That same summer, I found Hans Christian Andersen's *The Little Mermaid* at our town library in Alexandria Bay, New York. I looked forward to a tale of a beautiful mermaid finding her true love. Instead, the story made me cry: The little mermaid falls in love with a human prince she has rescued from a shipwreck and trades an evil sea hag her voice for legs of her own. When the prince marries a beautiful princess instead of her, the little mermaid is given the chance to return to her home—if she stabs the prince and his bride and smears the blood on her legs. She chooses her own destruction over killing the couple and joins the fairies of the air, gaining an immortal soul.

I remember thinking that *The Little Mermaid* was not a real fairy tale. Fairy tales had happy endings. Sure, Snow White and Cinderella struggled, but ultimately, they got more than they ever dreamed of. Andersen's little mermaid was nice and did everything asked of her, and still the prince didn't marry her. I didn't admire the little mermaid. I pitied her. My future would be better.

At age twenty-three, like Andersen's mermaid, I relocated for love. It didn't last long. My boyfriend soon moved out, and I ended up staying in our San Francisco apartment with my now ex-boyfriend's two friends as housemates. I watched a lot of television, alone. I worked as a high-school biology teacher. My students did not stare at me with wide-eyed wonder, writing down every word I said, as I had imagined. Instead, they asked for bathroom passes, often en masse.

The only thing my child self would have liked about my young adult life was that Disney finally released its animated version of *The Little Mermaid*. I saw the movie with another mermaid-loving girlfriend. In this version, the evil sea hag, now named Ursula, disguises herself as the beautiful rival princess. She tricks the prince into falling in love with her. In an action-packed conclusion, the little mermaid, now named Ariel, gets back her voice, vanquishes Ursula, and of course, marries the prince.

Disney made the fairy tale I longed for as an eight-year-old, but by young adulthood I had more in common with Andersen's nameless heroine. I don't know exactly why my boyfriend moved out, maybe he wasn't ready, maybe I wasn't the right person, maybe I was too clingy. What I did know was that he did not leave me because he was enchanted by an evil witch.

Today, deep into my forties, I'm married to a wonderful man. I also have a daughter. Like me, my daughter loves mermaids. As a preschooler, Chloe loved to hold her legs together and swish her tail in the bathtub, as she sang in a high soprano voice. I didn't mind the water on floor. I was glad Chloe didn't want to be a typical princess who wore a tiara over her coiffed bun. Chloe liked wearing her hair "mermaid style," loose over her shoulders with the occasional snarl. Chloe also loved swimming, no matter how cold the temperature.

Chloe was seven when I read Andersen's original story to her for the first time. She'd already seen Disney's *The Little Mermaid* several times.

"Hey, Mama, where are Ariel's friends, Sebastian and Flounder?" Chloe asked, halfway through the book. She pointed to the crab and blue-and-yellow striped fish figures on her bookshelf.

"They are not in this story," I said, and read a few more pages.

"Mama, this story is wrong. The Prince doesn't marry that bad girl that is really Ursula. He marries Ariel!"

"No, in the *real* story, the Prince does not marry Ariel," I said.

"I don't like this book," Chloe said. I sighed, and quickly read the final pages.

"Ariel dies?" Chloe sobbed.

I spoke slowly, hoping Chloe would appreciate Andersen's message. "The prince broke the little mermaid's heart, but she didn't kill him, even though she could have saved her own life."

"Mermaids are beautiful girls who wear pearl necklaces, and sing. They don't die," said Chloe.

Chloe insisted I leave her bedroom light on.

I should have expected that Chloe would dislike Andersen's story. In every story she had heard up to that point, when a hero or heroine took a risk, it paid off. Andersen's mermaid gives up her family, home, voice and fish tail for love that is not reciprocated. Rather than seeking vengeance, she accepts the consequences of her choices and gains a soul.

I reread Andersen's story to Chloe a couple of months later because I wanted Chloe to see that the real test of her character will be how she responds to defeat. I'm so glad I read Andersen's non-fairy tale at an impressionable age, preparing me for my post-college life, when little turned out as I envisioned.

But Chloe reminded me that I can learn from Disney's Ariel, as well. She is adventurous and optimistic, and she loves to sing. Like my eight-year-old self at the Saint Lawrence River, she doesn't notice the cold water.

After singing a rousing duet of "Under the Sea" at bedtime with Chloe, I decide to google Weeki Wachee instead of preparing my next day's lesson plans. It only takes a couple of tries to get the right spelling. The Florida roadside attraction has become a state park, and the mermaids still perform. I'm delighted that this part of my childhood has not disappeared. My mother was completely wrong about the bar-like atmosphere. Weeki Wachee now has camps for aspiring mermaids and mermen. During the day, the kids learn the daily responsibilities of being a mermaid, "while getting a behind-the-scenes look at what it takes to put on a show." Best of all, Weeki Wachee holds a "Sirens of the Deep" mermaid camp for women over thirty. During one weekend, participants receive underwater ballet training and get fitted for a mermaid tail. The weekend culminates with a private performance for family and friends. I click to register, but the camp is full. I'm not surprised. There is still room for fairy-tale magic in middle age.

Beth Touchette has taught science to high-schoolers, preschoolers, and everyone in between. Her personal essays about her children, travel, and pets have been published in the *San Francisco Chronicle, Marin Independent Journal, Denver Post* and KQED's "Perspectives." She lives in Northern California with her husband, son, daughter, overweight-but-dieting golden retriever, two canaries, and one hardy goldfish. She still wants to be a mermaid.

Literary Love

Sue LeBreton

I BREATHE AND RELEASE MY SHOULDERS INTO THE thick carpet on my bedroom floor. My legs are vertical, supported by the wall, and the soles of my feet face the ceiling. I do yoga while my thirteen-year-old daughter Abbey reads to me, the inverse of our norm. Tonight I have begged fatigue so she nurtures me. My eyes close and I let her deep, surprisingly big voice envelop me. In my mind I anticipate the precocious Anne Shirley of *Anne of Green Gables* solemnly promising to walk the ridgepole or perish in her attempt.

My mind wanders back to when I nursed Abbey. She was at my side in the football position, propped upon a semicircular nursing pillow patterned in pastel squares imprinted with baby symbols of rocking horses, soothers and safety pins. My book rested on my still-bulging belly. The two of us were wedged into the squishy, burgundy leather chair whose extra width embraced us. I read aloud from *Midwives* and *Where the Heart Is,* the Oprah's Book Club picks my sleep-deprived brain was picking its way through, hoping my voice would lay a foundation for a love of all things literary.

Two months later, for her first Christmas, I bought her the box set of the first three *Anne of Green Gables* books, and wrapped and placed them under the real Douglas fir tree, squeezed into the corner of our small family room, displacing the big, bur-gundy leather chair. My husband laughed, teasing me that despite how miraculous and advanced Abbey appeared to us, she could not yet read. The gift enclosed my deep desire that one day she would share my love of that story and all things book-related. I acknowledged that books are my go-to gift, noting the other volumes lovingly chosen for both her mater-nal grandmother and great-grandmother, who were visiting to share Abbey's first Christmas. Great-Grandma's eyes being diminished by macular degeneration meant that her gifts were now audio books. Three generations cuddled her and unwrapped the gifts for Abbey, each gift speaking to the hopes and dreams the giver coddled for this child.

The night she was diagnosed at eleven months, the oncolo-gist handed me a 500-page book about childhood leukemia. The sheer bulk of the book anchored me, offering me a sense of sta-bility while my mind whirled in a twister of disbelief and terror. They banished us from the intensive care unit with promises to page us if her condition changed. I clutched the book to me, my arms aching for the weight of my baby. We walked zombie-like to the family room we'd been assigned, a small, claustropho-bic room stuffed with a pullout couch, two flimsy end tables supporting nondescript lamps, a mass-produced coordinat-ing print on the wall and a beige, pushbutton telephone. As my husband and I lay on the couch-turned-bed, too stunned and scared to speak, I tentatively thumbed through the book. Titles like "Relapse," "Death," and "Bereavement" screamed at me from the pages. Pulling my eyes away those words, I forced myself to read about the author whose grown daughter had survived. Although my daughter's rare type of leukemia was not profiled in the book, I plodded through the introduction, hoping to absorb some of the terminology we would need to navigate this foreign land in which we had been dumped.

Weeks later she battled a fever and specialists paraded through the room all night long. I sat on a stool by her bedside, afraid to touch her because she was in such pain. Until now, screams had accompanied her pain and fear of needles and feeding tubes. This night she was silent. Her vital signs signaled intense pain to the professionals—pain in her head, her bones, her joints and organs such as her kidneys, liver and spleen as the chemo battled the leukemia cells lurking throughout her tiny, already shrinking body. Instead of sleeping in the portable, single cot where my husband and I took turns resting as we alternated twenty-four-hour shifts, I sat on a stool so that I was parallel with her body in the crib, and tried to read some *Maisy* books to her, thinking my voice might soothe her. But cheerful Maisy and her friends Tallulah and Panda could not pierce the chilling, deadly calm that surrounded Abbey. My reading made no impact on the monitors that displayed her racing heart. Thinking that silence might be easier on her senses, I read to myself. But my choice, *Angela's Ashes,* was the absolutely wrong book for my circumstances. Here was a story of a father who could not care for his child and here I was willing to do anything to save mine.

During the months we lived in the hospital I often sat in the windowless room, reading as she slept. My reading material morphed to magazines and humorous stories, pieces that helped my mind fly away from that cave-like room for small, precious minutes. When she was awake I read her favorite *Maisy* and *Bear in the Big Blue House* books to her, teaching her colors, shapes and words. On good days she would smile at the basket of books and point to the ones she wanted me to read, delighting me with her capacity to learn despite her illness.

Through the years I have watched with wonder as she learned to read, moving from one-word-per-page readers to the *Archie* comics I offered when it seemed that her interest in reading was stalled, to today's young-adult novels that we both enjoy. Along this journey I have sleuthed for any clue that might reveal cognitive defects from the chemotherapy but so far, none has surfaced. She lives a normal life with no memory of the devastating treatment. To help her understand how lucky she is, we recently read *After Ever After,* a book about a teenage boy who survived childhood leukemia but suffers from some aftereffects of the treatment. Although she is strong and healthy today, the shadow of cancer follows me. Every milestone, every shared experience carries that extra sweetness because it almost never was.

Now I lie here eleven years post-chemotherapy. I slide my legs down the wall and bring the soles of my feet together, switching yoga poses. My ear pricks up to Abbey's voice saying "Trish," pulling me into reality. Ah yes, it is not the *Anne of Green Gables* I had dreamed that we would one day read together. Instead, she's reading *Divergent* to me, a dystopian young-adult novel where the main character is preparing to fling herself off a building as part of her training. Perhaps it's not the classic material I had fantasized would be held in her hands, but the loving act is the same, the strong female characters perhaps not so different after all. I allow myself to sink into this yoga pose, sink into this moment, the daughter I dreamed of having, alive and well, sharing my love of reading.

Sue LeBreton loves to read aloud to her family while doing wall yoga. The unexpected challenges of her parenting journey have included cancer, autism, life-threatening allergies and diabetes. Through it all Sue has learned the importance of balancing self-care with taking care of others, and humor, lots of humor. When she is not writing, Sue is either working out, nudging her family into a healthier lifestyle, reading, encouraging others to read, or enjoying time with family and friends. She lives in Calgary, Alberta, with her husband, two children and two small, fluffy dogs.

It's A Boy

Leslie Lagerstrom

"I'M NOT RIGHT," MY EIGHT-YEAR-OLD CHILD WITH THE old soul explains, as to why our weathered mailbox sits empty. With another classmate's birthday party on the horizon, we wait anxiously for the invitation that never comes. Simple yet profound, the words slice through my flesh, piercing a hole in my heart, the pain more than I can bear. It is a pain I have come to know all too well, raising a transgender child.

It wasn't always this way, at least not in the beginning. With ten fingers and toes, a perfect Apgar score of 10 and no obvious birth defects, our healthy firstborn was cause for celebration. Yes, on that blue-sky August afternoon I delivered a beautiful baby who came wrapped in a blanket of hopes and dreams that were not meant to be. At least not as we envisioned those hopes and dreams when the doctor divulged the secret—"It's a girl!"—we had been patiently waiting to learn for the last nine months. No one in our delivery room that day, from the medical staff to my husband and I, would have ever guessed how wrong that statement would be.

From the moment of birth until our baby reached the age of three we lived in a state of naïve bliss, a magical land of new parenthood where we believed we were raising a girl. A beautiful little girl who would be Snow White on Halloween, wear

89

red velvet dresses and matching patent leather shoes during the holidays and go by the name of Samantha. Never mind the fact that this child preferred Matchbox cars to Barbies and bull-dozers instead of baby dolls. Society had graciously given us the "tomboy" label to justify her behavior, which we gladly used as a wishful excuse. But all too soon it became hard to ignore the earnest pleas for the McDonald's Happy Meal that included the boy's toy or the innocent requests to wear male clothes, right down to the boxer shorts underwear. These were pleas and requests that occurred daily as our child tried to tell us, in the only way she knew how, that there was a disconnect between her mind and body.

"You are pioneers," we were told, the tone implying we should be proud, as we met with the first group of doctors to discuss the gender atypical behavior we knew extended well beyond "normal." Pioneers because, as we quickly learned, there was very little research and data on transgender children. I remember my mind flashing back to *Little House on the Prairie,* a favorite television show from my youth about pioneers and their hardships, which seemed oh so simple compared to what our family was now facing. Pushing through the mounting fear, not because we were brave, but because we knew the physical and mental well being of our child depended upon it, we hitched up a team of doctors—internists, endocrinologists, psychologists and psychiatrists—and began to plow the field of medicine searching for answers to help our child become whole.

Over the last five years Sam, as he is now known, has endured innumerable pokes and prods to his body and soul— puberty-blocking drug injections and seemingly baseless psychobabble questions—so that he can be the person he has always known himself to be, inside and out. At the same time, our family has embraced that pioneer spirit, plowing not only the medical field, but also the field of education to ensure our child is safe at school. Working with teachers, we have circled the wagons to combat the daily attacks of harassment and bullying from fellow classmates who lack empathy and derive pleasure by inflicting emotional pain.

Equally important, our family has learned to be advocates. Appearing in front of medical professionals, school officials, friends, fellow students and parents, we stand side by side with Sam as we explain a subject that is unfamiliar to most people and misunderstood by society at large. With every opportunity to share a glimpse of what it is like to walk in his shoes—shoes that are well worn because of the rough and uncharted road he has already traveled in his short life—we feel encouraged knowing one more person might go forward with a new appreciation and understanding for people like Sam. Indeed, nothing prepares you for the challenges of raising a transgender child, but with unconditional love and acceptance we believe we are showing our child and everyone who knows our family that gender alone does not define the person.

Leslie Lagerstrom is a proud mom of two children. In 2011 she created the blog *Transparenthood*™, which chronicles her family's experience raising a transgender child. Through *Transparenthood*, Leslie has been able to lend support to parents who find themselves in the same situation while also helping spread awareness on the subject of gender variant/transgender children. Her essay "It's A Boy" was a finalist in the 2012 Notes & Words essay contest. A graduate of Iowa State University, Leslie is at home in

Minneapolis, where she enjoys downhill skiing with family and long walks with her faithful dog Molly.

Demolition and Creation

Cynthia Lehew-Nehrbass

THE BULLDOZER CONTINUES ITS ONSLAUGHT OF DIGS and smashes. Brick by brick the exterior walls tumble into heaps and scatterings. My petite teenage daughter looks up at me with hands guarding her hearing aids from the repeating beeps and crashes outside the window. Sarah moans and makes her special sign for "loud" by wiggling fingers aside her earlobes. I pull her cheek into my waist, cup her forehead with my palm, and hush her. Her body softens as she snakes an arm around my hip. And, there we stand, side by side—across the street and five stories above the entrance to Minneapolis Children's Hospital   watching its annihilation.

I glance down at my daughter. Just above her shirt's neckline is the top of a pale scar that runs down the middle of her chest—stretched taut and lengthened by a decade and a half—the souvenir from an unwanted journey. She touches it with her fingertips. Does she know that this is the hospital where she received the thickened vertical line that neither time, nor salve, has managed to mask or fade?

"Do you remember this place?" I lean forward and ask her. Surely she must. She searches, as if she expects me to say more, cocks her head and then traces an index finger down her right cheek—the sign for "sad." No tears wet my face, or even well in my eyes. My expression feels heavily impassive. Yet, her keen barometer of my feelings is spot on, and I believe she perceives the profound heaviness in my stomach, the tightening of my throat, the sense of loss, unexpected.

I've carried the weight of this place on my shoulders for nearly fifteen years. I've cemented into my life the fear that I have my daughter only on borrowed time, on loan from machines, from death, from God; and at some point I'll have to give her back. Memories of this hospital, Sarah's surgery, the twenty-four hours of unfathomable limbo between life and death, waiting for her six-month-old grey heart to beat again, my struggles with faith—all have been lain, with skillful masonry—into the foundation of the mother I've become. Every decision made, every second of worry, hovering over a daughter with special needs and a sick heart, began in this place. My inability to separate the fret of loss—the sorrow of what might have been—from the fullness of joy that is my daughter: it's all paved and bonded here. And yes, you would think that when she survived—the miracle, the gift—that I'd have shaken it all off, moved on, only celebrating. This is how I desperately wanted it to be. I'm smart enough to know that no good can come from the baggage one carries on such isolative journeys, yet I continue to shoulder the tonnage of that day.

Sarah leans her face towards the glass, pulling me forward with her. She points toward the angular crane. The driver, in his plexiglass cage, pivots the wheels about face, swings the arm of the truck's shovel and forces an awning to fall with one giant pummel. Beams screech in their letting go—succumb to force, surrender to change. For decades, this roof has held the burden of rain and sun off those who keep vigil for sick children.

It has been as welcoming as any roof could be. But, now, look how easily it disappears, the only trace of its past in mere remnants of fractured frame and gutters. How long will it take to forget the swallows that nested and circled in the hollow above the bench where my mother had sat, in need of air that day, and where her brother from Montana had arrived, unexpected, in a taxi, to meet his dying grandniece? The shade of those chestnut brown beams is now the color of disintegration. I worry: *Did the birds find new homes before the loss of everything?*

When the particles finally settle, the faint outline of a window comes into view. It looks into an intensive care room—Sarah's. I know how unlikely this is, but I strain the yards of my vision, past dust and mortar, to glimpse inside. Time collapses, and I see the shadow of the massive ECMO machine, standing guard at the foot of Sarah's bed, still pumping—removing, oxygenating and replacing her blood with continuous swirls—and me, hovering over my splayed and tube-invaded child, praying.

I don't know if I fully understand fate, or the tease of irony. But I do respect life's timely metaphors. It isn't just that we happen to be there that particular day, at a random appointment, watching, as the structure that held critical memories in my life is being rendered obsolete. It isn't just that for months I've told myself that I needed to revisit this place, to recheck its visual markings, seal sensory details into my mind so as to write this place into memoir. And it isn't just that I've begun to doubt my ability to capture in words the significance this place had in my own transformation, or its power over my body: how the scarlet hue of the chapel's carpet cushioned my anger at God that day as I fell to my knees, or how the constant smell of iodine triggered waves of nausea, how the stagnant hospital air sucked all moisture from my skin, or how the sounds of alarms and ventilator pauses played tricks on my own heart, causing it, too, to skip beats.

How is it that, years later, here I stand with my daughter securely behind the glass window, observing from afar, to bear witness to the passing of a reality into mere memory. The wheels of the truck, in its struggle to back up in the rubble, make a grinding noise, but all I hear are the faint whooshes and whirls of the pumps that once kept my daughter alive, the nearly imperceptible shuffle of doctors and nurses making their rounds, and the whispers of family members asking, over and over, if I need anything, while against me, Sarah leans, her breath warm, and her complexion far warmer than the purple paleness of my baby with a broken heart. Dear irony, I see you've come to play amidst the cracks and crumblings of these walls.

For a moment, Sarah's face twists in confusion, then she laughs a sudden, "Ha, ha!" I try to figure out what she finds so funny. Few memories from the hospital cradle such humor. She giggles again with raspy delight. Perhaps it is the "dozer," a giant version of the "digger" in the park that she loves to sit on, pulling and pushing the levers, enjoying the power of reorganizing the earth. Or it could be that the truck is now stuck, a favorite new word in her slowly growing vocabulary. Sarah wiggles her fingers under her chin—the sign for dirty—and states, as assuredly as if she'd globbed ice cream onto the kitchen table, "It's a mess." She does not have the same grave foreboding, or even regret about this place, as I do. She is simply enjoying the breaking down of this building with the ease of toppling blocks. There is joy in its destruction, the potential for something new to be erected in its place.

I nod and kneel down beside her. As if it's a secret to be shared only between us, I whisper, "This is the place where I thought I'd lost you forever."

I don't know why I say this. Perhaps a need to acknowledge the bigness of the moment, the significance of what we were witnessing or, maybe, I want to give a eulogy to a place that has been such an important part of my past. Or perhaps, I mean to say to my daughter, *Come with me, my companion in this journey, validate the power those shards of glass, that bent steel, a mound of dirt, still have over me.*

She turns her face toward mine and smiles. Her hazel-browns hold a confident "I know" look, impish, playful. Although she was only an infant when death nearly stole her from me, her eyes tell me she remembers it all. "Silly Mama," they seem to say, "Here I am."

No, my daughter isn't mocking my memories with her beautiful smile. Despite her innate innocence and her inability to fully comprehend many things of this world, in the realm of emotional awareness she is unbelievably perceptive and wise. Her insightful gaze recognizes, and calls to attention, my complete inability to let my sorrow and worry go.

Those memories of heaven's hold on Sarah's life (the visual details of every minute nearest death) are still so palpable that I cannot imagine a single tool of destruction—not even bull-dozer or crane—that could render them benign. No hours of therapy, no years passing, no counting of blessings, and no strength of will. My most useful tools, save God's grace, are pen and paper, the keyboard and screen. Wise teachers have guided, "Write about this; write of that." And so, little by little, I must chip away at memory's fortress with chisels of words and empty spaces. This is the only true way out for a writer, isn't it? I will write and wait for that transformational healing to begin, for the fog to dissipate and memories to relinquish their hold. Yet, all I can really say is this: *My daughter nearly died* (and this is the truth), *and it changed me forever.* Truth again.

I've been told that the chapel, the family waiting area where my husband cried in my mother's lap, and the tiny parent sleeping room, with its narrow chair-bed—where we took shifts resting in the darkest of hours—are all nearly gone too, crushed or remodeled beyond recognition. Changed forever. I regret this. I want to write of these spaces in order to be rid of the power they have over me; and now they are gone. I can no longer revisit them. Yet, I cannot imagine their absence for they are as real to me as they were then. My memory's curse, a writer's blessing.

So this is where it begins. As the walls of the hospital change, I'm called to carve sentences out of this place where my daughter's heart was stopped and the moment God started it again. To find the perfect phrasing – placing commas and dashes in the expiratory pauses of that mountainous climb within my faith when I realized that I, alone, could not save my daughter. I must craft scenes from the jumbled truths and doubts that have followed me all these years, sift through their nuggets of wisdom and bits of insignificance, and then put final quotations around my own voice. The chapel and waiting room can vanish, and I will still need to pen some poetic reality about how it rained the day my daughter's chest was opened with scalpels and clamps, about the ebony sky, void of white and fluffy cloud, that released sheets of rain to wash all faces that turned towards heaven. In the blackest of ink, I will admit that there were no windows where I waited, no scent of fresh air or spring dampness mixed with exhaust and evergreen, no sound of precipitation pelting car and concrete, or thrash of leaves on wind's howl, no view of bending blades of grass or birds in search of cover; that I could only feel the pressure of unseen molecules concave my shoulders and neck—like a weighted backpack on a climb to Everest—so thin was the air that day. Yes, this entrance and its overhang can crumple, and on the page I will become that mother sparrow circling her nest, waiting to carry her daughter through its front door and safely home.

Sarah and I stand by the window for nearly twenty more minutes as we watch the last of the demolition and the dump truck come to receive the rubble onto its back. I wonder where the window and wall pieces will end up, if they will be recycled; if the concrete and metal scraps will be finely processed and reused for other structures, or other rooms. If so, will they bear any resemblance to the shadows of the chapel, or the white wash of the waiting room? Will any of the experiences that happened within those walls find their way to other buildings, other lives; better yet, will they finally release themselves from mine?

I take Sarah's hand and sign, "all done," like at the end of a movie. The truck is leaving with its fill. We have yet to make it to our appointment. Not to her cardiologist, this time, but a normal teenage checkup. Surprisingly, there is so much that is typical, and so much that is still special, within our unique journey.

When Sarah and I finally leave, it's with the realization that it is right, and fitting, that I was able to witness the tearing down of the hospital, while standing next to my daughter. It is right, and fitting, that I can still hold her hand and walk away from the window, with her. It isn't fate. It isn't irony. It is just the beginning and the ending of a personal metaphor. I know this.

And so, I will pick up my pen, and let the memories have their way with me. With each syllable and white space I will give new home to where they might reside. From this demolition of place can finally come something new: the creation of our story, built from toppled bricks.

Cynthia Lehew-Nehrbass is a multi-genre writer, choreographer, dance-studio owner, teacher, and mother of two teenagers. She holds a degree in dance performance and choreography from the University of Wisconsin and a certificate in creative nonfiction from the Loft Literary Center in Minneapolis. She has published essays in the anthology *Windows Into Heaven, The National Down Syndrome Congress Newsletter,* and various online publications. Her daughter (the subject of her current memoir project) was born with Down syndrome, a congenital heart defect, and hearing loss.

The Mother in the Square

Jessica O'Dwyer

IT SOUNDS LIKE THE PERFECT VACATION: SIX MONTHS alone with my then fifteen-month old daughter Olivia in a rented casita in charming Antigua, Guatemala, a country so beautiful that guidebooks call it the Land of Eternal Spring. And it might have been, if Olivia were legally mine, and not the baby girl my husband and I had spent all of 2002 trying to adopt. Tim and I couldn't understand why our agency had cashed our $12,000 deposit check and skipped town, or why, twelve months into it, we hadn't progressed past the first step.

I was one of eight American would-be moms living in Antigua. Married and single, straight and gay, we hailed from California, New York, Arkansas, and Wyoming, with little in common save our desire to become mothers and the belief that our bureaucratic nightmares should not be suffered by anyone else. Each of us had quit a job to focus full-time on sorting out a stalled adoption. Mornings, we'd load our kids into baby joggers and wheel them to the Internet café, where they played together in the courtyard while we plotted strategies to get them home: the senators we planned to lobby, the latest letter we wrote and to whom, the bribes our facilitators had urged us to pay. As we sat comparing notes on our progress or lack thereof, the other mothers used to say, "Somebody needs to write a book about this."

My entire life I'd been searching for the one story I had to tell. Even as I was living the ordeal, I knew Olivia's adoption saga was it.

For more than twenty years, I'd supported myself by putting words on paper, in magazine publishing and as a museum publicist; but like many English majors who punch a clock to pay the bills, I secretly yearned to pen a page-turner. Here, finally, was my chance. The universe had presented me with a harrowing plot, complete with exotic locale and complicated, compelling characters. With my husband's enthusiastic support, I decided to stay home with Olivia and, while she napped, dedicate myself to writing our memoir. Yet every time I turned on my computer, feelings of panic and loss overwhelmed me. At night when I tried to sleep, I was haunted by bad dreams—that someone had kidnapped Olivia, that she was drowning, that our house had caught fire and she was trapped inside. To guard against the emotions that remembering evoked, I kept reorganizing my notes and reading tomes that outlined the history of Central America. I wrote the same twenty pages over and over again.

Worse, those twenty pages fell completely flat. While living in Antigua, I'd been too preoccupied to take precise notes of the town's physical details, the landscape I'd seen, the people I'd met. I hadn't figured out how to communicate the essence of what it felt like to be me, alone with my baby in a foreign country, terrified that I may lose her. To reconnect with those feelings and details, I needed to return to Guatemala.

I hadn't been back in three years, and that time I traveled with family. Now, I would go alone, and of course I would stay in Antigua. Whatever I needed to discover, I believed I would find it there. As soon as my taxicab turned off the main road from Guatemala City and drove through Antigua's ornate colonial gate, I knew that I had.

I was right back in the world of our story. Cobblestone streets, típica markets, a ring of volcanoes, handmade tortillas. The pool at Hotel Antigua, the crowded aisles of La Bodegona supermarket where the boys who bagged groceries remembered my name. I visited Paola, our housekeeper, and Lila, who taught me Spanish. Climbed the steps of the cathedral. Sat on a bench in the square.

When I returned to my hotel room at sundown, I couldn't write fast enough. I needed to record every detail. The red geraniums in the courtyard. The door knocker shaped like a crouching lion. The sweet scent of the orange chocolate bread that came out of the oven at Doña Luisa's at precisely three p.m. The exact location of the shoe shiners at the mercado.

The next morning, I woke with the roosters, and left the hotel in search of breakfast. The sky was turning pink as I headed toward my favorite restaurant, the one attached to the Internet café where the other mothers and I had met daily with our babies. Few people were on the street. As I reached the edge of the square, I saw a lone American woman pushing a baby jogger, walking in my direction. Like me, she was dressed in jeans and a T-shirt, with blonde hair pulled back in a ponytail. Her skin was as pale as mine. In the jogger slept a Guatemalan toddler, around fifteen months old.

As the woman approached, I felt a shock of recognition. The lined face with a strained expression. Blue eyes filled with fear and defiance. Hands clutching the baby jogger, as if to say, "I'm the mother of this baby. No one can take her away." The woman was me. She was all of us.

My heart began pounding as I saw how defenseless she was, how vulnerable, yet how bravely she marched forward, protecting her child. Tears sprang to my eyes, and I knew I had broken through. Whatever it took, I was going to write our story, not only for me, but for her, and for every other adoptive parent. For our children's birthmothers and foster mothers. For our children themselves.

Somebody needed to bear witness to our experience. I was the one who lived it. The task had fallen to me.

Jessica O'Dwyer is the adoptive mother of two children born in Guatemala. Her book *Mamalita* (Seal Press, Berkeley) was named best memoir by the San Diego Book Awards Association and one of the top five books of 2011 by *Adoptive Families* magazine. Her essays have been published in the *New York Times, San Francisco Chronicle, Adoptive Families, West Marin Review,* and the *Marin Independent Journal;* they have aired on public radio and won awards from the National League of American Pen Women. Jessica is a vocal proponent of open international adoption and lifelong connection to birth country. She speaks frequently on these subjects at Heritage Camps, adoption support groups, and book clubs.

Shut Up, Shelly

Janine Kovac

WHEN I READ THE AD FOR THE WRITING CONFERENCE in Napa Valley, I started salivating. Four days in wine country. A stellar faculty of editors, agents, and authors, including two Pulitzer Prize winners. Quaint accommodations that featured rustic cabins, a pool, hot tub, and organic meals. A Yoga for Writers class. This was the writers' retreat for me!

But then I read, "Bay Area's first juried writers' conference" and "only 40 spots," and my shoulders slumped.

"You'll never get in," Shelly said. Shelly is the cranky old critic who perches herself on my shoulder and looks down her nose as I write. She is embarrassed by my work and encourages me to delete sentences before I even type them.

"This conference looks like the kind of place for capital-L *literature*," Shelly snorted. "You write 'mommy memoir.' It's not the sort of thing the judges are looking for. Besides, you don't even have a decent writing sample to submit."

I had this one essay I'd written the previous year for a contest, the theme of which was "unforeseen challenges of parenthood." I thought my story about giving birth to premature twins would be a perfect fit.

The piece didn't get any traction—not in the contest, not in the motherhood magazine that sent a request for original childbirth stories, not in the spoken-word Mother's Day event.

"I told you so," Shelly said, each time a rejection floated into my inbox.

But *I* liked my essay. It was the first thing I'd ever written about my boys that carefully balanced the often-tragic facts of our situation with the emotional truth of it. And each time I gave it to my writing group for feedback, I remembered something else about those early months in my boys' life. I wrote about vivid images such as the eerie green glow of the hospital equipment at 3:00 a.m. and the plaster cast of the boys' footprints that were barely bigger than my thumbprint.

With each revision, Shelly muttered, "People don't want to read this stuff. You're not going to get in." But my inner writer didn't care. My inner writer thought, "This essay's my baby. You don't like my baby? That's OK. I like my baby." This time I was writing for me, not for what I thought other people wanted to read. So I kept writing.

I revised the final paragraph over and over—the scene in which I held one of my sons for the first time. I wanted to capture in words the warmth and weight of holding a tiny, fragile newborn. The sweet scent in the swirls of my son's damp hair. The way he squeezed my finger in his sleep when I whispered to him. Each rewrite got a tiny bit closer to that sensation, rooting my memories in concrete phrases. And the closer I got to capturing those scenes and emotions in words, the further Shelly and those judges drifted away. Sure, I wanted to get into the conference. Of course I wanted people to like what I'd written. But I was the one who'd lived it. In that sense, I was the best judge of what was good in my writing and what was not.

Nineteen drafts later, I uploaded my essay. The piece that had started out as eight hundred words had blossomed to three thousand. When I hit the "submit" button I felt a swell of pride. I'd written the story I wanted to write and I'd kept revising until I felt like it was the best essay I was capable of. Even Shelly thought it was pretty good by the end.

Six weeks later I got a congratulatory email from the conference organizers. Two months after that, the essay won third prize in a national contest for *Pregnancy and Newborn* magazine. I read an excerpt from the piece at Litquake, San Francisco's literary festival. It was great. It was all great.

But with each accolade and acknowledgement, Shelly still had something to say. When I got my acceptance letter for the conference, she told me that the other writers there would look down on me because mommy writing is not serious writing. (Not only was Shelly wrong, but it turned out that *all* the writers at the conference were worried that their writing wasn't "serious" enough.) When I won third place and saw my article in print, Shelly got all huffy because she thought third place wasn't good enough. And when I read at Litquake, and the reading was so successful that I was invited to read the piece at another literary event, Shelly whispered, "But what if you never do this well ever again?"

The only thing that shut Shelly up was the writing itself. When I wrote, I saw my sentences in terms of truths. (Are these words true to my experience? Are they true to my voice?) Shelly, on the other hand, only thought in subjective terms of "bad," "good," and "not good enough." But sentences aren't really like that. Sentences either work because they drive the narrative forward or don't work because they're driving the story someplace else. When I look at my work with regard to emotional truth, I don't care what Shelly has to say. She still mutters on and on, but my words on paper speak louder than her doubts.

I don't think I'll ever get rid of Shelly. Right now she's stalking me because we're waiting for a rejection email for a writing residency in the Pacific Northwest. She's still reminding me how we didn't get that writing grant for parents and she can't imagine why anyone would want to follow me on Twitter. But at least she stays out of my writing studio—unless it's to give her final approval to something I've written. For example, right now she's nodding her head. She thinks the line about Twitter is a nice touch.

Janine Kovac is also the author of the essay "The Next Prompt."

Backseat Writer

Meghen Kurtzig

I BLAME MY OBSESSION WITH WORDS ON BEING THE firstborn child. I was shy and reserved while my younger brother and sister were loud, rowdy, and always in motion. Books allowed me an escape from their constant interference.

Once, I did try the swift application of a book to a sibling's head but I found that actually reading the words and jumping into the story better suited my escapist purpose. Reading was particularly helpful during interminable road trips where my personal space was measured in centimeters. I would read and wish to be elsewhere. Somehow it worked—I gained the extra centimeter of space I needed, and saved us all from backseat bloodshed.

My firstborn status qualified me to be the bossy big sister and I considered being a know-it-all as a huge compliment. My poor siblings were subject to its full force, since I didn't speak much to anyone else. I took my role very seriously. After all, I was the keeper of information. I was happy to tell them what to do and how to do it even though they mostly ignored me. The occasional rare moments when they responded as if they wanted to know more spurred me on. My teaching skills became more polished and I enjoyed providing instruction. I was reserved in conversations and social situations, but when it came to imparting information, I was the kid bouncing up and down in my seat. I wanted to talk. I wanted to teach.

Now, as a mother at home with two children, I am no longer shy, but still a little reserved. I find myself again in need of some magic words in order to make it through the day. My family is wonderful but they are also loud, rowdy, and always in motion. So, I continue to find my centimeters of peace through reading.

But I need more. I need the excitement of putting words on the page. The challenge of pulling the right words together and shaping them into something interesting. I write about things I'm knowledgeable about as well as things I imagine, and I hope that I don't sound like a bossy know-it-all.

Meghen Kurtzig, RN, CNS, is a parent educator, nurse, and aspiring writer. She gets inspiration and hugs from her two children and support from her wonderful husband. Meghen is the finance chair for the Write On Mamas. She is also the creative editor for the Southern Marin Mothers Club magazine. When writing alone doesn't offer enough space from reality, Meghen writes fantasy fiction. If there is any free time left over she'll swim, bike, and run but prefers not to do them together.

Dear Baby #3

Jennifer Van Santvoord

I HAVE HIGH HOPES THAT AFTER YOU ARE BORN I WILL write about your every move: Your first smile, the first time you will sit up, roll over, crawl, and walk. But let's face it. You are Baby #3. I'm sorry about that. But when there are three children in the family, someone has to be third (and in our case, quite hopefully, last — no offense). The youngest child is notoriously overlooked and underrepresented in baby books, photo albums, etc., and while I wish I could say that won't happen to you, there is a reason for that notoriety, and unfortunately I can't make any promises.

So these high hopes I have are tempered by realism. And after hanging around your brother and sister for the last five years, I have learned a thing or two about expectations: Don't set them.

When you become a parent, you will understand that *nothing* happens the way you expect it to. Want to get your son to school on time? Sorry, it's not gonna happen. You'll spend half the morning asking him to get dressed for the day. You'll ask politely at first. And when that doesn't work you'll ask him again, this time a little more forcefully. And then . . . again, even more forcefully. You'll try negotiation, coercion, and finally begging (ok, YELLING), before you'll see any actual pajamas being removed or daytime clothes being put on. And now, just like that, you are fifteen minutes late for school. Again.

Want to catch up on that book you've been trying to finish reading for the last six months? Uh-uh. Your entire evening will be consumed with refereeing the impromptu children's boxing match that breaks out in your living room, and now that post-bedtime "me time" is taken up with all the tasks you wanted to accomplish three hours before.

Want to wake up early to go to that amazing yoga class? Yeah, right. The night before, your children took turns throwing up, every hour on the hour, and now you're too tired to remember your own name, let alone how to do downward dog.

Finding time to write about you will be an uphill battle, for sure, little one. But it will make all the times I *do* write that much sweeter. I will feel so incredibly accomplished when I write . . . anything. It may not happen often, but it *will* happen, and that's what counts. So while the frequency with which I will write about your milestones and hilarious idiosyncrasies may not quite compare with how often I wrote about your brother and sister's, I will still write. I have to, because writing is what has allowed me to stay sane these last five years, and I am going to rely on it that much more when that third variable (a.k.a. You) comes along.

So my promise to you is this: I will always strive to equally represent you in my writing, just as I will promise to love you equally. You just have to promise to provide me with good material, as I'm sure you will. I have no doubt that your adorableness and antics will inspire much of what I have to say in the coming years.

Now, there is a solid chance that someday, when you are a teenager, you will resent the things that I have written about your childhood, especially if it involves stories of you running around naked, lighting things on fire, you know, that sort of thing. I expect that. You're supposed to be angry with me all the time, and think I know nothing, etc., during that stage in your life. But I hope that some day, like most young adults, you'll come around, and realize that your mom actually did know what she was doing, and that what I gave to you with my writing was really an invaluable gift, a record of who you once were, and how much joy and laughter you brought to my life—a gift that, hopefully, you will cherish for the rest of your own life.

Love,
Mommy

Jennifer Van Santvoord is also the author of the essay "The Write Identity."

Intervention

Joanne Hartman

WE'RE HAVING A BREAKTHROUGH DISCUSSION ABOUT an ongoing problem, my daughter and I. At this moment, she's calm and open to talking with me.

"You know, if used responsibly and in moderation, it can be a good thing," I explain. Her head tips toward mine, and I let it rest on my shoulder.

"It is a privilege, not a right," I add. "If it interferes with other things . . . "

"But I just can't help it," she sighs.

I nod in understanding. I was once there, too.

This is good progress. Isn't the first step recognition of the problem?

Flashback to minutes earlier and things are not this calm.

"Stop that reading thing!" I cry, and reach for my seven-year-old daughter's treasured book.

"Don't ever take it away from me!" she sobs.

"If you can't read responsibly—" I tell her.

"I can so read and eat!" she yells back, denying the problem that has made her late for school daily, now, for over a week.

What to do? As it is with many problems, I begin by thinking of quick, little fixes. For example, I've long ago given away our stash of sippy cups, but lately I've been wishing I'd kept just one. How handy it would be right now.

Because this is what happens: She tilts her head sideways to reach the mug she's drinking from—she knows the milk will spill if she tips it toward her mouth, so her mouth instead tips toward the cup, not once averting her eyes from the page. Milk trickles down her chin, so she stops even bothering to drink. She's reading, and all other activities are merely annoyances, pulling her away from the task at hand. Eating, drinking, sleeping—done only because we insist that she must.

The Reading Thing also keeps her up too late at night. She reads *Harry Potter* while brushing her teeth, even while changing into her clothes, which slows these tasks to such a lengthy endeavor that they become Herculean in nature. And I miss her, dammit: her full and complete presence and those sweet conversations we used to have before she started sticking her head in books.

"Bookie, bookie," she calls in mock baby-talk for her beloved object if she realizes it's not with her, as younger children cry out for blankies or favorite toys. She runs to where she might have left it. It's her favorite thing, her passion, the thing she does not want to do without.

I empathize with this newfound love for reading, and I am glad she's hooked on something that will open many doors for her. I smile when she yells out, "Listen to this, Mommy!" and then shares a particularly witty passage or well-worded phrase, knowing that I will love it, too.

Yet, it's starting to concern me, the intensity of the infatuation. Does she, perhaps, read too much? Is this the beginning of an obsession that might get out of hand?

She's genetically predisposed. She comes from a long line of obsessive readers. My father read Bill Clinton's thousand-page autobiography in six sittings. My grandmother carried books of Yiddish poetry in her purse, ready at any spare reading moment. And I know now that I've done damage by my own example. She has seen me so many times, during the seven years I've been her mother, bent over a book and ignoring the world around me, the ringing phone, the dirty dishes. It's my respite from a far too busy life.

I also hold myself responsible for her habit by being her codependent. I bring her book into the car as she requests when I could just as easily say, "Oops, forgot it!" If I had, then she wouldn't have missed the deer family of five that flew across the road. I even aid and abet by procuring not only the books themselves but also helpful reading tools—magnetic bookmarks and a metal book stand, so now she can read hands-free.

Lately, The Reading Thing has become a problem in other unanticipated ways. Normally my daughter is a lively companion and full of creative energy, but during a recent play date at our house, she stood up from the pretend-we-have-a-whole-lot-of-kittens game she was playing with her friend—they were disagreeing as to where the kittens' bed should go—and announced, simply, softly: "I'm going to go read."

The friend looked up, surprised, unsure of what to do. This withdrawal from social interaction comes unexpectedly. I looked up from my *New Yorker* and jumped into action; this incident necessitated an impromptu lesson in reading etiquette. I quickly listed the dos and don'ts of reading in the company of others. Designated, mutually agreed-upon reading time: okay. On a play date when the friend doesn't want to: absolutely not.

After the play date (which we did cut short by a bit), we read together for the rest of the afternoon, I finishing up my magazine, she completely absorbed in *Harry Potter*. I don't know how much longer she'll be happy reading next to her mother, so I'm enjoying this while I can, the two of us curled up together, our legs entwined, our minds lost in worlds beyond, doing our favorite thing.

I guess I shouldn't have been surprised the next day when she announced that reading is far more interesting than school. I flash forward to her as a bookish teen, one whose giggling friendships are a thing of the past. I wasn't one of those teens—opting out, distant, sitting in the school library. I did read, but usually at home or on the bus. At school, I loved being with my friends and I want this for her, too, to be able to separate her reading life from her friendships, and not miss out on either one.

I list the positives of her school—mention her friends there by name, the felt gnomes they're sewing in class, the fort in process by the creek. I joke, facetiously, "So, you just want to stay home and read *Harry Potter* all day?"

She looks up at me, her eyes wide with hope. "Could I?!"

Sure, I get it; she'd rather be in Divination with Madame Trelawney, peering into crystal balls, or growing baby mandrakes in Herbology class. I'm sure this is not a unique problem among *Harry Potter* readers who attend non-wizard schools.

I've felt that way, too, not about Harry because he hadn't been written yet, but about Meg in *A Wrinkle In Time* and the *Bobbsey Twins*. I wanted to hang out with them, join in their adventures, be part of their world. I tell her this. I explain that Harry will be waiting for her after school, on her booster seat, which is such a strange image that I actually take a photo of the 870-page book laid open to the page she's on, just as she left it on her car seat that morning.

I'm sure that I'll look back on the beginning of her reading obsession with fondness and pride. I don't know where it will lead, although its passionate and early start bodes well for its continuing. It may be just a phase or, perhaps, the beginning of an everlasting habit she'll have to learn to balance with the other experiences of life.

As we wait to find out, I can at least vow to be a better role model and read less often, at least when she can see me. I'll pick up the ringing phone. Schedule designated reading time. Put on a timer. Remove the book stand from the kitchen counter.

And if all this fails, I might just go out and buy her that sippy cup.

Joanne Hartman is a freelance writer and editor who lives in Oakland with her husband and daughter. She is a founding member and profiles editor of *Literary Mama* and former columnist for San Francisco's *j. the Jewish news weekly of Northern California*. Her writing appears in the *East Bay Monthly*, *Interfaith Family*, and the anthologies *Literary Mama: Reading for the Maternally Inclined*, *Using Our Words*, and *The Knitter's Gift*. Prior to motherhood, Joanne worked for a New England public television station on an award-winning feature magazine show, was a reporter and photographer for a sailing magazine, an editor at a wire service, and spent a decade teaching middle school. Her daughter, now a teen, happily balances The Reading Thing with The Math Thing, The Guitar Thing, and The Hanging-Out-With-Friends Thing.

Giving Birth to Creativity

Marianne Lonsdale

I SPENT MOST OF MY LIFE BELIEVING THAT I WAS NOT creative. When others would talk about their artistic endeavors, I'd laugh and say, "I don't have a creative bone in my body." The artistry of others fascinated me—dance, paintings, music, literature. I was an avid fan, but not a participant.

When I was a child, the only artistic activity I was allowed was tap dance lessons. I practiced in the garage, slapping my taps on the grey cement, always veering off course into my own choreography. But when I was six, my mom pulled me from class. I was crushed that I had to quit before dancing to the song "Turkey in the Straw" at the annual recital. I had two younger brothers, and Mom needed my help. Making good grades and completing household chores were what was important in my family. Most everything else was deemed frivolous.

I grew up surrounded by families from church, from school and from the fire station where my dad worked, but no one involved with music, drama or art. We occasionally had art classes in my Catholic grammar school, taught by a single mother who rode a motorcycle to school, her son in a sidecar. Creativity was for weirdoes.

And yet, I told short stories before I knew my alphabet. My parents nicknamed me Bird's Eye because I was always observing and commenting on what I saw. I hated the nickname. My older sister was Princess. Who would want to be Bird's Eye? I doodled poetry during my first years of grammar school, but my stories were considered similar to crayon drawings; only a few ended up in the manila envelope where my mother stuffed keepsakes of my childhood. By fifth grade, I believed that my stories and poems were a waste of time.

So instead, I read constantly. Not many kids knew there was a whole series of Oz books or that *The Addams Family* was originally a series of one-panel cartoons in the *New Yorker.* I read them all, and talked my way into getting approval for early entrance to the adult section of the public library.

But still, I ignored my urge to write until college when I enrolled in creative writing. I figured I would finally discover the keys to the kingdom and would meet others who valued writing.

Out of my high school class of 558 students, only about 10 of us earned admission to four-year colleges. This was not our world. No one in my family had graduated from college, and no one wasted time in a writing class.

But I hoped to find my place, to define my space in that creative writing class. I slid into a desk at the back of the classroom. Fifty men and women, most of them much older than I, clustered in desks in front of me. Some flirted with each other, something I admired but had no idea how to do. I was an awkward and shy teenage girl. Some students were writing away in notebooks—already writers.

The teacher explained that our writing would be critiqued by her as well as our fellow students. Heat flooded my face. I didn't know how to get words started on the page—and even if I could, I was way too self-conscious to let anyone, especially these people, read my words. I never wrote a word and never returned to that classroom after that first day.

I lost the desire to even try to write. I didn't know how to, and accepted I was not creative. I was no different than anyone else in my family.

Decades later, when I was forty-one years old, along came my one and only son, Nick. His birth sparked a creative lust. I'd sit up in bed, my back resting against pillows, nursing my son, looking down at his dark mop of hair, filling his hunger, while feeling my own need to express more than breast milk. I knew my son was leading me somewhere new, but where was not clear. Creating this beautiful little boy made me feel like I could create other things. And that I must.

For the first few years of his life, this urge to create came out in the form of scrapbooking and a drawing class in which the teacher explained that he could teach us how to draw. By this time I was older, wiser, and inspired.

I was soon drawing at home, in parks, on vacation. I didn't care who saw my drawings. I liked the way time slowed while I worked my pencil. It was weird, but by focusing so intently on whatever was right in front of me, I made the present seemingly disappear. I'd get lost in a flow of creativity, a meditative state. This was similar to what I'd felt with my newborn baby and I wanted to keep it going, to grow it.

On Mother's Day, the year my grey-eyed son turned four, my mother gave me that manila envelope stuffed with mementos from my childhood: report cards, class photos, crayon drawings. And two stories I wrote at eight years old, carefully typed for me by my twelve-year-old brother. A memory of early creative passion flooded my body. I'd loved writing, and I recognized that little girl, that funny, imaginative imp I'd left by the wayside as I'd matured.

I enrolled in a creative writing class at the same adult night school where I'd taken the drawing class, and lucked out again by finding a marvelous teacher, Charlotte Cook. She always found something good in everyone's writing. Even in pieces I'd be hard-pressed to like, she would find a great story, or great paragraphs in need of a story. Always something seemed to surprise her, to awe her.

The students discussed my first personal essay in our second class. My stomach muscles were pulled so tight I could hardly breathe until Charlotte said, "We have a writer in the room—what an amazing piece." I was stunned.

I moved from the public adult school to a private weekly workshop in Charlotte's home. I was still terrified when my pieces were critiqued, and although the group's approach was supportive, I'd leave feeling wiped out. But I was drawn back every week—to my writing and to the group. I tried my hand at short stories and could almost imagine a novel. Two years passed before I could listen to the group without wanting to run from the room.

About that time, two women in my weekly group were accepted to the Squaw Valley Community of Writers, a prestigious weeklong conference held every July in Lake Tahoe. I was stunned that they'd even applied. Were we good enough to be doing that? Were we really writers?

I applied the next year, submitting a short story for the fiction group and a personal essay for the nonfiction group. Although I expected to be rejected, I was still crushed when the email notice arrived that confirmed my expectations. I'd told no one, not even my husband that I was applying, so at least I did not have to admit that I'd been rejected to anyone. I was rejected again the next year. And the next year. And on my fourth try, I was accepted. Persistence paid off.

The Community of Writers at Squaw Valley was everything I'd hoped for and more. By the end of the first day, I felt more like a writer than I ever had in the nine years I'd now been writing. The attitude of the faculty was that if you were there, you were a writer. I felt like I'd finally joined the club. Talking about writing for a full week was exhilarating. Karen Joy Fowler, author of *The Jane Austen Book Club,* led the workshop critique of my novel excerpt. Other big-name authors hung out with us all week: Anne Lamott, Mark Childress, Jason Roberts, Dagoberto Gilb, Janet Fitch, Amy Tan. It was like Hollywood for me. I applied again the next year, was accepted again, and had an equally amazing experience.

I'd been slow to call myself a writer. My childhood view of art as frivolous still popped up and I'd be embarrassed to tell family and co-workers that I wrote. But those two visits to Squaw Valley caused a shift—I started taking myself seriously as a writer.

Which means that I scheduled time to write—no small feat since I have one of those corporate gigs that will take over your life and your soul if you let it. I used to feel I was taking time away from my husband and son when I wrote, so I'd wait for the rare occasion when they'd both be out of the house and then try to conjure up my muse and get my fingers moving on the keyboard, even then feeling guilty that I wasn't cleaning out closets.

I now sometimes write in the dawn hours, sometimes I go to the library on Tuesday nights (the only night the libraries in

Oakland are open—sad state), and sometimes in the waiting area at my gym after a weekend workout. And this year— strike up the drums—I am taking a weekend to myself almost every month to keep my novel moving. I write this piece from the Courtyard Marriott in San Ramon—only thirty minutes from home—a quiet respite where my creative muse can stretch and play.

And what I love (aside from how much more I'm producing now) is that my now sixteen-year-old son is growing up in a home that values time spent on creative projects. He sees me sometimes choose a morning of writing over a morning of housecleaning. We hang out at Peet's Coffee together, his head buried in homework and mine busy crafting my novel.

Literary Mama published a blog post of mine a few months ago. In it I described how my son had inspired my writing career. I read it aloud to him when it was published. His grey-blue eyes welled up and he hugged me tight—not something that happens often with a teenager. He knows now that he's my inspiration, my first and best creation, and that any time he wants to draw instead of emptying the dishwasher, he's got my okay.

Marianne Lonsdale writes personal essays and short stories, and is now focused on developing a novel. Her work has been published in the *San Francisco Chronicle, Literary Mama, Fiction365, The Sun,* and *Pulse.* She's read at various events including San Francisco's Litquake festival. Marianne is honored to be an alumna of the Community of Writers at Squaw Valley. She lives with her husband, Michael, and son, Nicholas, in Oakland, California.

Slide Show

Mary Hill

I SLID MY SKIS FORWARD TO THE BLACK RUBBER LINE
and glanced to my left to make sure my twelve-year-old son
Oscar was keeping up. He was shuffling along slowly, slipping
back two inches for every six inches forward. His instructor
from the disabled ski school had assured me that he was ready
to ride this lift—they'd ridden it together just that morning—
but my jaw tensed watching him. Was I pushing too hard?
Expecting too much? Oscar's skis finally reached the line, and
my husband Paul and my other two children glided in beside us
just as the chairlift swung around. I sat down on the black vinyl
bench and then reached up to clutch Oscar's hips and guide his
bottom to the seat before the lift lurched forward. But I realized
too late that I also needed to straighten his legs. His right ski
caught on his left and disconnected from his bright red boot. I
twisted around and watched the ski slide across the path of the
lift, almost tripping the next group of skiers on its way down
the bank.

I sighed. "Don't worry Oscar, someone will bring it to the top,"
I said, sensing his panic even before the words reached his lips.

"How do you know?" he asked, his voice shrill with worry.
His anxiety lurks just under the surface and pops up in the form
of endless questioning whenever uncertainty or overwhelm

arises. (*How did I know* his ski instructor would meet us at the fire pit? *How did I know* these were his poles?) My older son Abe sensed my impatience and chimed in instead. "Oh, it happens all the time, Oskie! It happened to me yesterday. I can see the lift guy handing your ski to someone now." He used his sing-songy chipper voice, the one he reserves especially for calming Oscar. It worked.

"Really?" Oscar replied, giggling.

I leaned back then, scooching my shoulders in between Oscar and Ruby, my youngest, and breathed in the cool Sierra air. I gazed around at the enormous green pines standing tall against the deep blue sky and felt my anxiety and impatience dissolving. And then it occurred to me. I peered to the right, over Ruby's head toward Paul, and then to the left, over Oscar's head to Abe. And I counted. Five. All five of us were there. On the ski lift. Together. I clenched my jaw and swallowed, trying to keep the tears that were prickling at the corners of my eyes from flowing freely down my cheeks.

"Paul, we have to take a picture!" I cried out. I looked ahead, hoping we'd have time before we reached the top. Paul chucked off his gloves and dug into his anorak for the camera. He stretched out his long arm and we quickly huddled together and smiled.

But we both knew the picture wouldn't tell the whole story. That photo of our family of five smiling on the mid-mountain chairlift won't tell how, just as we were heading back onto the slopes after lunch, Oscar screamed at Abe for gliding over his ski, causing him to fall. It won't show Abe's gentle apology or how Oscar's face turned purple anyway and his hands sliced through the air wildly as he yelled, "It's all your fault, Abe!" while Abe cringed with embarrassment.

It won't show how just three minutes before getting onto the lift Oscar snowplowed down the gentle slope toward the chair, right into another family. He banged into the mom's pole and landed sprawled out on top of their skis, trapping them. I showered them with apologies while Oscar lay on the ground, crying and unable to get up. Oscar looked to Paul, his red face scrunched, and screamed, "Dad, it's their fault. They didn't get out of the way! It's all *their* fault!" Paul's mouth tensed and his voice sharpened as he told Oscar that he needed to apologize, no matter what. That you can't blame the people you run into. Ever. Paul turned to me then and revealed a rare sadness.

"Here I thought it was so cool that we were heading off to ski together," he said quietly, "like we finally reached this family milestone, and then he has a major meltdown in front of all these people."

And the photo certainly won't tell how later that same day I spent two hours trying to get Oscar down the mountain before dark. Oscar slid backwards down a steep section while I was checking the trail map. I pulled him back up to a flat spot and he flopped to the ground in a tangled mess of skis and poles. He screamed that it was *all my fault*. A young boy stopped abruptly to avoid Oscar and accidentally sprayed wet slushy snow in his face. That was my fault, too. Eventually we started to ski again, but just five minutes later Oscar started shrieking that his legs were in pain, and that he couldn't go on.

"*Mom,* there are pins and needles jabbing into me," he screamed. "I can't move! Ow! It's so painful!" I begged and cajoled but Oscar wouldn't budge.

And the photo won't show how, finally, defeated, I called Paul, who insisted on trekking halfway across the mountain to find us. Oscar stopped shrieking, knowing his dad was on the way, and we sat on the snow scouring the shadowed peaks for Paul's tall, graceful-only-on-skis frame. Paul arrived a half hour later, smiling, immediately easing Oscar's anxiety. He shimmied Oscar up onto his back and skied him down, making wide careful turns while I followed behind with three sets of poles. We arrived at the bottom just as the ski lifts were closing, the sun so low that Paul and Oscar's long shadow resembled a two-headed giant with pencil-thin legs.

But most importantly, that photo of our family on the mid-mountain chair won't tell how, when those tears had started prickling at the corners of my eyes, I was instantly transported back to the darkened NICU (neonatal intensive-care unit) room where five-day-old Oscar lay motionless in an isolette, unable to nurse or cry. Paul and I were huddled around a computer, staring at a list of diagnostic criteria for the terrifying genetic disorder our doctor feared he had. My legs started to shake uncontrollably as I recognized every one of Oscar's puzzling symptoms on the list. Low muscle tone. Weak cry. Poor sucking reflex. Downturned mouth. Undescended testes. And as Paul scrolled down to the list of Prader-Willi syndrome characteristics that appear later in childhood, the room started to spin and my knees buckled. I gripped the counter and lowered myself onto the tall, circular stool. Developmental delays. Cognitive impairment. Behavioral challenges. Short stature. And the scariest one of all—insatiable appetite. People with Prader-Willi syndrome never feel full and do anything to obtain food, including, I read, rummaging through dumpsters for discarded scraps and breaking into neighbors' basements to gorge on frozen meat. The words swam on the computer screen as

I struggled to understand. Craters instantly appeared in the once solid path I thought our life would follow, sucking my typical parenting dreams down into their deep holes. Violent tantrums, locked refrigerators, rigid thinking, skin picking, mental retardation—none of this had been part of my plan.

But now, twelve years later, that floppy baby in the NICU isolette, the one who couldn't stay awake or turn his head, the one we feared would struggle so much with food and behavior that we'd never be able to even go on vacation, was skiing. Skiing! And even though that afternoon on the slopes was far from peaceful, even though we attempted something far above Oscar's ability, I was brimming with pride and full of hope that next time Oscar would make it on and off the lift smoothly. Next time he would ski down the mountain. Someday he would be ready to tackle the blue runs. After all, that morning at Squaw, Oscar had happily donned his heavy parka and jammed his feet into the rigid boots, when most days he refused to don anything other than his well-worn sneakers. He'd schlepped across the expansive parking lot carrying his poles and had beamed confidently at his ski instructor. After six years of lessons he'd finally graduated from the bunny hill and skied on green runs at the top of the mountain. For the first time ever he agreed to ski with the family after lunch. And he did—I swear—manage at least one snowplow stop without running into someone.

A few weeks before our ski trip I read an article online about special-needs parenting which highlighted a diagram that the mother of a young boy with a rare genetic disorder had drawn to illustrate her child's care network. At the center of the diagram was her family, and lines spidered out in every direction connecting them to some seventy plus medical professionals, teachers, therapists, attorneys, family, friends, and information and support organizations. I nodded and sighed with tears in my eyes as my own spidergram sketched itself in my head. Sometimes even I forget what it requires to raise a child like Oscar. I'm used to educating teachers, friends, and family about the dangers of unexpected or unauthorized food. I'm used to anticipating stressful situations so they don't trigger emotional outbursts. I'm used to attending tense educational meetings with seventeen or more teachers, therapists and specialists to advocate for the appropriate school placement and services. My calendar is filled with medical appointments, and the thick binder I cart to every one has a color-coded tab for each of the various specialists he sees – gastroenterologist, endocrinologist, pediatrician, orthopedist, dentist, and ophthalmologist. The filing cabinet in the corner of our bedroom contains several drawers full of Prader-Willi syndrome research articles plus the last three years of educational reports, assessments, and goals. (The previous eight years' worth are stowed in another filing cabinet in the basement.)

At the bottom of the article there was a slide show—pictures of the boy riding a horse, sitting in a canoe with his sister, hitting a ball off a tee. As I scrolled through the pictures, my jaw started to tremble. Tears rolled down my cheeks and splashed onto my keyboard. Aside from the captions, there was little about those pictures to indicate that this beautiful child had special needs. And yet I knew that each picture told a deep and complicated story. Did this mom ever dream her son would be able to ride that bike? Or agree to wear that heavy riding helmet? What about climb into that wobbly canoe, and know not to stand up or topple overboard? Does she spend hours emailing and coordinating all these activities, making sure her son has the emotional and physical support he needs to participate? Does she, like me, burst with pride over these simple ordinary accomplishments, things I take for granted with my other children?

My own slide show is chock full of pictures like hers. Oscar wearing a snorkel mask in Hawaii. Oscar just off the zip line in Costa Rica. Oscar buzzing his bumblebee wings in the fifth-grade play. And now I will add the photo of our family on the ski lift to my slide show. I will post it on Facebook. It will star in next year's holiday card and all of our family will celebrate this milestone with us.

But the pictures are just not enough. They can't tell the whole story of how we navigated that crater-filled path that lay before us in the NICU. Our life is not as we expected or hoped, and there are still major craters that we skirt around on our journey with Oscar. Several years ago I started writing to tell the stories the pictures could not, to document and remember the joy and heartbreak that exist simultaneously when raising a child with special needs. My son will never play on his school's basketball team, go away to college, or have children. He won't even ever buy his own groceries or drive a car. But he does bounce alongside me on our walk home from the school van stop each day, chatting away about everything from the latest music his classmate shared with him to the attributes of the various Chinese emperors he's learning about in history. He plays jokes on me, and closely monitors the batting averages of his favorite professional baseball players. He started a dog walking business and can ride a two-wheeled bike. He even has a girlfriend. Typical twelve-year-old milestones, yes, but hard-fought in a child like Oscar.

I scribble these small victories (and all it took to achieve them) down on Post-it notes, on the backs of crumpled receipts, and, if I am lucky, into a blank document on my laptop, not wanting to forget these joyful moments that I never dreamed would exist. And as the words fill the page I see some of those craters fill in. Even those stubbornly deep ones, like independent living and unlocked cabinets, lose a little of their importance as the paths around them widen with other meaningful possibilities.

Oscar was exhausted after our stressful afternoon on the ski slopes that day. Relieved that we made it down safely, we meandered dazedly through the packed parking lot to the car. I drove him back to our rented chalet, peeled off his many layers of clothing, and settled him into his bed with his favorite stuffed giraffe for a much needed nap. And then I raced up to my room, opened up my laptop and typed as many details as I could remember about our misadventures on the slopes. I didn't want to forget a moment of it. I knew others raising their own children with special needs would find humor and comfort in our crazy tale.

But underneath all the anxiety surrounding our descent down the mountain there was also a burgeoning pride and undeniable hopefulness that Oscar was almost ready for that challenge. It's that hope I wanted to remember most, to someday share with all those new moms staring at their own terrible list in a darkened NICU room. And, I admit, I also wanted to store those memories in case someday the challenges of PWS become so overwhelming that we find ourselves trapped by newly widening craters blocking our path. Craters that we can't just hop around, or avoid with a well-planned detour.

There are no guarantees, I know, that Oscar will continue to do so well. There are no guarantees that we will always be able to provide an environment in which he can thrive.

And so while I will continue to snap those photos for my slide show, I will also keep writing the stories that accompany them, hoping they will provide encouragement for others and maybe, someday, needed solace for me.

Mary Hill is the mother of three, a writer, and a medical and educational advocate for her middle son who was diagnosed at birth with Prader-Willi syndrome. Her essay "Gone" was a semi-finalist in the 2012 Notes & Words essay contest. Her essays have appeared in the national and California Prader-Willi syndrome association newsletters as well as several disability-related blogs and newsletters. Some of her writing lands on her own blog, *Finding Joy in Simple Things,* but most sits on her hard drive waiting for her to polish it up and submit it.

There Was a Before

Teri Stevens

Tears stream down your face when you lose something you cannot replace.
—"Fix You," Coldplay

THERE WAS A BEFORE.

I am reminded of it every time my three children and I go to the library to "buy" books. You see, across the street and a few doors down is a funeral home, Treadway and Wigger Funeral Chapel. The kids don't even know it's there or what it is. But I do. I was there once before—before we were blessed with a beautiful, healthy, happy son whom we adopted from Guatemala and brought home when he was just six months old, and before we were doubly blessed with twins who were carried to term by my sister because my breast cancer meant that I could not.

In other words, before our lives came to appear idyllic to those on the outside looking in, there was great sorrow.

I remember being in pain. This was nine years ago. It was a Thursday. I had been in pain for four days. I had gone to the doctor that Monday, but he couldn't find anything wrong and said that the pain I was experiencing was most likely due to fibroids. Since I was in my twenty-fourth week of pregnancy, six months along, he advised me to take Tylenol. I didn't. I remember thinking that the pain could be caused by Braxton Hicks contractions, about which I had recently read.

At the time, I was the marketing director for the Napa Valley Opera House. Continually on the computer writing press releases, answering emails, or putting together one of the many marketing collateral pieces the job required, I would grasp the arm of my chair whenever I felt pain coming on.

My husband, Bill, was out of town on business for the week. Since I was feeling so awful, I decided to go to bed early that Thursday night, thinking the pain would subside if I just lay down. It didn't. I called my doctor at about 9:30 p.m.

"It's Teri Stevens," I said into the phone. "I'm in a lot of pain." I let him know what had been happening since Monday's office visit, the grasping of the chair, the bending over in pain every now and then when I walked.

"Well, if you think it can wait, I can see you in the morning." He sounded tired. "Or you can go to the emergency room at the Queen. It's your decision."

I said I'd see him in the morning and hung up. I lay in bed grimacing and thought, I'm going to get premature wrinkles if this continues. I got up to use the restroom, but once there my body felt like pushing, not like urinating. Not a good sign.

"Don't worry little one," I said to him or her, "it will be okay." We had chosen not to find out the sex until the birth, but then for some reason, the thought *I'm going to name you Jeffrey* crossed my mind.

"Don't worry, Jeffrey, it's going to be fine. You stay in there," I coaxed. Maybe by talking, I was trying to calm myself, tell myself it was going to be okay.

I knew I had to go to the emergency room, but didn't think I should drive myself, even though it was only two miles away. I called 911 and asked them not to use sirens; I didn't want to wake the neighbors. I was struggling to put on my shoes when the doorbell rang. The fire department arrived first, in a quiet truck, red light flashing a bright circle of alarm in the dark. At the door, a fireman helped me put on my second shoe and then the two men picked me up and carried me down the few small steps to the driveway and put me on a waiting gurney. The ambulance had arrived. I remember tossing my keys at one of the firemen, asking him to lock the front door. There was a light spring rain. It was February 18, 2005.

I don't recall the ambulance ride, but I do remember the bright light of the stark white hospital room they wheeled me into. Someone removed my glasses. I wasn't there for more than a few minutes when I gave birth to our son. I remember pushing myself up on my elbows in an attempt to see what was happening.

"Is he okay, is he breathing?" I asked the doctor and nurse who were moving quickly, talking together in hushed tones, their medical jargon going over my head. Without my glasses, the room was a blur and all I saw clearly was the look on the face of the ambulance paramedic who turned away from what was happening at the end of the gurney.

"Yes, he is breathing," someone said, but then he was whisked away to the NICU. I didn't get to see him. A nurse was cleaning me up from the birth, which was so fast, I was simply numb. At the time the thought didn't cross my mind, but has many times since, what if I didn't call 911? I would have had Jeffrey at home, by myself, the outcome of his life in my hands. It would have been the same, but it would have been my fault.

My doctor arrived. Someone had called him. "I am sorry, Teri," he said quietly. "Your son did not make it; his small lungs were not developed enough. Just one more week and it could have turned out differently." I didn't say anything, just cried. I felt deflated, all the hope I had that it would be okay, gone. I remember thinking that just days before I had read in *What to Expect When You're Expecting* that babies born after twenty-four weeks can and do survive. So how could this be? For whatever reason, the pediatrician on call made the decision not to step in and try to save his young life.

I didn't want to call my innocent husband, sleeping in a San Diego hotel room, with this life-altering news; I wanted him to sleep. I told the hospital staff that I would wait until morning. Ultimately, the doctor came in with a phone and gently prompted me to call.

"Hi, I'm sorry, I know it's the middle of the night, I'm at the hospital, something terrible happened. The baby was born early, it was a boy and he didn't make it."

Shock on the other end of the line. "What? How?"

I looked around the hospital room, unable to believe I was having this conversation.

"I was in pain, I called 911 and I wasn't in the emergency room for more than a few minutes and I gave birth," I explained through my tears. Bill told me he was so sorry and that he would be home as soon as possible and asked to talk to the doctor. I don't remember what was said. Thankfully, I fell asleep, escaping the reality of what happened for a short time.

I remember the nurses telling me what a beautiful baby he was, that his hair was blonde, like mine. It just didn't look like that when the nurses brought him in to me, since his head had been bruised from the quick delivery; I thought his hair was dark, like his father's.

Later, while I was lying in a hospital room alone, there was a knock on the door and an older woman who was some sort of grief counselor came into the room. She sat at the side of the bed and told me she was sorry for my loss.

"Don't lose hope, it will get better, spring always brings new life after winter," she fiercely said, as if her tone had the ability to make me believe. Usually a polite person, I turned away from her attempt at comforting me and asked to be left alone.

And then Bill was there, crying with me and holding my hand, sorry that he had been away. Before coming to my room he had met and held our son. What he thought in those moments, I'll never know. I told Bill I named him Jeffrey, after my cousin, who had passed when we were children.

Before I was discharged, I asked to see Jeffrey again. Bill thought it might not be a good idea, but I was adamant. I had experienced so many emotions in such a short time: fear that I would give birth; heartbreak that I did too soon; guilt that it was my fault; loss of the child I would never know. I realized I should have been spending time with the one I would never see again. He was so tiny, dressed in baby blue, lying in a small basket. I kissed his cool forehead. So did Bill. Our goodbyes.

In the dark months after Jeffrey passed, I never thought I would have a family. These thoughts were compounded when we did get pregnant a few months later, only to lose the pregnancy due to complications. And then I was diagnosed with breast cancer. My whole being was saturated in grief. I am grateful that ultimately I was determined to create a family, and had the support of a loving husband who was open and willing to pursue other options.

Today I feel that somehow, even though he is gone, Jeffrey was looking out for us. Two years and one day after Jeffrey's due date, our adopted son Alex was born. And then, three years and one day after Jeffrey was born and passed, his sisters, Emerson and Mikayla were born. Which means, strangely enough, that right now I have three children who are all six years old.

I watch their heads bob up and down as they peruse the children's library DVD section. I think about Jeffrey and wonder how different my life would be had he survived. Certainly it would be full and rich. But it would be different.

Jeffrey is not here in the physical sense, but through writing about him and the family that resulted from his presence, I am able to make some sense as to why he isn't here, and to keep the memory of my son Jeffrey Thaddeus Stevens alive.

There was a before. But now there is also an amazing and full after.

Teri Stevens lives in Napa, California, with her husband, son, and twin daughters. A graduate of the journalism school of the University of Nevada, Reno, Teri is the program coordinator for Girls on the Run Napa Valley. She is a founding member of the Write On Mamas and serves as the group's marketing director. In addition to writing young-adult fiction, Teri writes about parenting her three six-year-olds.

The Dry-Erase Author

Maria Dudley

I STAND AT THE FOOT OF MY DINING-ROOM TABLE WITH eight middle-school kids patiently looking on. The topic of my Writing for Home Schoolers class today is how to write a watermelon seed story. I hold up a quick crayon sketch of a red watermelon slice with little black seeds drawn in. "Back in my day," I tell them, "watermelons weren't seedless. Eating a watermelon thirty years ago was a lot more complicated than it is now." It's my version of "When I was your age, I had to walk ten miles to school in the snow."

I explain to the students that when you start to write a story, personal or fiction, you want to start with a detailed small moment. Instead of telling about your whole day at the beach, you will instead tell about the driftwood boat you assembled with your cousin. I worry a little bit that they are too old for this crayon drawing and cutesy explanation of how to write with detail and focus, but the kids seem to enjoy and understand it.

On the whiteboard easel I begin writing my own watermelon seed story. My writing is a little bit messy and slants down the whiteboard even though teachers are supposed to have careful printing. The story is about the time that I was eight years old, and my dad wanted to take me on the huge wooden roller coaster at the Santa Cruz Beach Boardwalk. I write that because I am too scared to ride this roller coaster, I kick off my flip flops, hoping it will make me just short enough to stay under the measurement line. I tell the middle-school students that it is details such as this, and the description of the sticky-sandy ground under my feet, that will help them to be better writers. Still, I always worry that the examples I choose for them aren't good enough. It's hard to write in front of others, even children. But I hope that if I do it, they will too. It's important for them to see examples of writing in action, and I talk aloud to myself to show them my thought process. The children also enjoy getting a little glimpse into my life and my children's lives.

Then I walk around the table, encouraging the kids to write down their own stories. I want them to write with honesty and humor. Sometimes they get stuck, but often they produce one-of-a-kind stories about teasing their five-year-old brothers into believing there is an actual Batman cave nearby, or learning how to use chopsticks for the first time, or how their uncles convinced them that if they don't secure their socks somehow in the middle of the night, the sock monster will steal them.

Sometimes people will ask me, "As a writing teacher, what do you write?" At first I tell them that I am so busy teaching that I don't have time to write, but then I remember that I write every day in front of my students. I write a small story and then I wipe it away to make room for some lesson on how to use quotation marks or semicolons. Most of the writing I have done in the past three or four years has just been erased away.

I realize I could write on butcher paper in order to make a permanent imprint, but it's too bulky and awkward to store. I have a green journal which gets moved all around the house in hopes that I'll use it daily or nightly (but I just can't find the time). It's a cute and clever journal—the cover is made of a discarded and recycled library book with the old-fashioned check-out card page still included along with some of the original pages scattered amongst the new blank ones. The man who makes these journals simply goes by "Doug," and I want to support Doug by buying new journals from him every year at charming arts-and-crafts festivals. His company is called Recover Your Thoughts. I would very much like to recover my thoughts rather than continue erasing them away, but in the end, the whiteboard is where I write.

On a recent trip to Nepal with my husband and my two sons, I learned about a kind of art that gets wiped away. At one point we visited an art school in a Buddhist village where they taught *Thanka*, a religious form of painting. As we walked around the art studio, students painted *mandalas*, colorful and intricate paintings in a circular pattern. In the corner of the room there was a *mandala* made entirely of sand by gently pouring millions of grains one color at a time onto the template to create the piece of art. After a *mandala* is completed, a ceremony takes place, and then the entire piece of art is brushed away.

It's like a giant Etch-a-Sketch, which I think is cool because who needs a giant room full of art?

After the ceremony, the sand is placed into an urn; half is given to the audience, and half is placed into a nearby body of water. It is believed that the sand will continue on to the ocean, providing a healing blessing to the planet. The sand *mandalas* are actually a metaphor for the impermanence of life, which is one of the essential doctrines of the Buddhist philosophy.

I've always liked the Buddhist doctrine of impermanence. I find it extremely comforting to think about how natural it is for things to change. I think about this in terms of my kids all the time. Others might see them growing up faster than I do—it's always someone else who first notices the little boy munchkin voice turning into a man's voice—but I know that it is happening. My older son is a freshman in high school this year, and I feel sad to think that we have only three more years with him before he goes off to college. When my younger son entered sixth grade this year, I suddenly felt old. My little boy was moving on, just like my students move on every year. I notice this kind of impermanence often. The writing that I do on my whiteboard in my teaching may seem not at all permanent, but in many ways it really is.

A while back I wrote a story for the students about the time that I was ten years old and in a sailing program. Part of our instruction required us to sit in a small sailing dinghy, tip it over into the cold bay, get it upright again, and then try to climb back in the boat. It was called getting your "guppy" award. The kids really liked hearing that story. I didn't exactly understand why, since it seemed like a fairly mundane detail of my childhood. But a year after that story appeared on my whiteboard, an adorable, spastic, never-does-his-homework student of mine remembered it and mentioned it in class while we were all brainstorming for topic ideas. "Like that guppy story, Mrs. Dudley!" he said. If I initially thought that my erased words weren't captured anywhere, I might have been wrong.

So we start with just the seeds, the small moment stories, and even if we erase them, even if we let those words disappear like the *mandala* sand to the sea, they're never really gone.

They may be reshaped and recreated later when my students tell their own stories, just as Doug reshapes old library books into new pages for new stories. So, even though I continue to wipe away my stories, I will keep writing them.

Maria Dudley has been an elementary and middle-school teacher in the San Francisco Bay Area for over twenty years. She teaches writing classes to home-schooled students and finds that most of her own writing gets erased from the whiteboard she uses in her classes. Maria has had a passion for books and writing since childhood, and was an English major at UC Berkeley. She is a wife and mother of two boys in Walnut Creek, California. Every night she forces a poem on the family at the dinner table.

Writer's Block Retreat

Claire Hennessy

I WAS DRIVING INTO THE BACK OF BEYOND WITH THE top down, music blasting and a massive smile on my face. Arriving in Middletown, California, in the late afternoon sunshine, I found my destination nestled in the valley below Mount Saint Helena in Lake County. I was staying in one of three charming wooden huts in the large, meadow-like garden of a typical California ranch house. My room had a lovely light and airy feel to it due to the large skylight directly over the bed, which would be ideal for my main purpose but not, as I was to find out, for sleeping past sunrise.

Fed up with my complaining about not having enough time to write, my mum and two sisters had clubbed together and bought me a stay in this idyllic spot, so I could complete the final part of my humorous memoir about how my husband and I had met at boarding school in a leafy English suburb on the outskirts of London. I had been a mere thirteen years old and he had been my first boyfriend, but then we had not set eyes on each other for over thirty years until we reunited after a chance email.

I had been looking forward to this weekend for months. I was desperate to finish my book, as an editor had read my unfinished manuscript recently and seemed interested. As each week went by without penning more than a couple of pages at most, I would say to myself: "Never mind, you have your writing retreat coming up in May," and I would feel a bit better.

I took out my laptop and looked at it, all shiny and blue, ready and willing to help me produce my bestselling masterpiece. How I had been yearning for some peace and quiet, all by myself, to write. No distractions. Just me and my keyboard. No husband, no kids, no pets. Deliberately, I turned off my Internet and silenced my phone. It was time to write. Finally. The time had come. My time. Just me and my trusty computer. No sound but the birds and the humming of my computer. Heaven. I sat, fingers poised over the keyboard, ready to burst forth with creative musings. And . . . nothing.

Nada.

Zip. Zilch. Zero.

My brain was blank. Completely and utterly blank. I didn't know where to start. It had been so long since I had last written anything that I wasn't in the same place, either emotionally or physically. I got up and walked around the garden and then tried again. Still stuck. Perhaps if I read a few more chapters . . .

I opened up the massive ring binder I had brought with me. As wisely suggested by a fellow Write On Mama, I had printed out a copy of my entire manuscript. She had told me that seeing a printed copy made her realize how much she had achieved already and encouraged her to finish her book. It was definitely good to see and touch the pages, over 200 of them, a great big chunk covered with neatly typed words. I had written my book in four parts and I only had the final part to go. I had lots of notes and some chapters were partially written, but the whole book needed a strong ending, with all the loose ends tied up. I opened an email from the editor and reread her thought-ful comments. One of her notes mentioned that there didn't appear to be a resolution to the antagonism between my sister and my husband, and she wanted to know what had happened to cause the friction between them. I sat and thought about that for a while. Why had Sue hated Bug so much at school when she hadn't even met him? Why had she called him The Black Deathwatch Beetle?! It had been a mystery all these years.

She was my older and much more outspoken sister whom I adored and had always looked up to, but I had never just come out and asked her what her problem was with him. Why didn't she like him, even now after all these years? He was kind and funny and clever and interesting. At least, I thought so. I didn't relish the thought of bringing up this very touchy subject. God, get a grip, Claire, I said to myself, just call and ask her. You're fifty years old, for heaven's sake!

Finally, after watching the clock relentlessly tick away my precious writing time, I decided not to be such a wimp. After all, what's the worst that could happen? Taking a deep breath, I gathered up my courage and Skyped her home number. After a couple of minutes of chatting about how lovely the accommo-dation was, she asked: "So, how's the writing going?"

"Oh, um, err," I uttered eloquently. "Actually, that's why I'm calling. I, um, I'm a bit stuck. One of the comments I had from the editor who read my manuscript was about you and Bug and why you don't like him very much. She wondered why."

I stopped and waited, holding my breath. Would she be furious I had brought the subject up? Would she turn it back on me somehow? Would she tell me something I didn't want to hear? Maybe I should have let sleeping dogs lie.

"Oh," she said, sounding a bit taken aback by my question. "We're okay now, I think. That's all in the past. I've moved on and I think Bug has too."

"Yes, I know things are better between you now. But why didn't you ever like him before?" I'd started this conversation and I didn't want to stop without getting some sort of an answer.

There was a long pause. I put my hand over my mouth so I wouldn't say anything.

"I don't know," she replied finally.

"Oh," I said. More silence. I felt awkward, but forced myself to push it a bit more.

"You don't know?" I questioned gently. "Surely you must know why you hated him so much."

"Well, no, I don't actually," she responded a little sharply. "Maybe it was a past life thing. Maybe we were enemies in a previous life. Who knows? Why don't you just make something up?" she said, as if that was a perfectly reasonable suggestion.

Sitting there a bit frustrated after the call, I thought about what she had proposed. Make something up? But then it wouldn't be the truth, or at least the truth as I remembered it. Could I change my book to be a sort of "fictional memoir"? Slowly, the idea started to take hold. Why not have it based on a true story, but not all the truth? As long as I told everyone up front, surely that would be okay. I thought about that for a bit. There were other issues that could do with a bit of creative license, like why my stepdaughter was so hostile toward me. My writer's block brain began clanking into gear. Images flashed across my mind. I pulled open a notebook, grabbed a pen and started writing.

Immediately I saw my antagonistic stepdaughter as a Goth, dressed all in black clothing, black leggings, black T-shirt and black army boots, covered in piercings with heavy black makeup. She was quite often in a bad mood with me so I thought of her as a bit of a "black cloud" at times in our new, blended family. My daughter, already painfully thin and a bit finicky, I decided would have an obsessive-compulsive personality with an eating disorder. Maybe bulimic, vomiting all the time in unexpected places, like the laundry hamper or behind the sofa. My son— well, that was easy, I would just exaggerate his Harry Potter looks and his nerdy behaviors. He could already bore for Britain on "Doctor Who" and other sci-fi programs. My two stepsons were not in the book much but I was sure I could make them funny and interesting. My mum I would make into an adventurous, thrill-seeking, plane-flying danger junky, always off on one terrifying jaunt after the other. My dad would be a control-freak wine snob—but wait, how was that different? My younger sister was a Buddhist nun already so maybe I would just make her extremely devout and rigid, perhaps always going on about the virtues of a chaste existence, and how sex is just messy and dirty and creates drama and attachment. So that just left my husband and my older sister. How to sort out the conflict between them?

When my husband arrived as prearranged, to take me out to dinner early evening, he found me head down, scribbling madly in my notebook in a slightly frenzied manner.

"How's it going?" he enquired, putting his overnight bag on the bed and giving me a kiss.

"How do you fancy being a long-haired, hippie drug dealer?" I asked him.

"What?" he laughed, looking confused. "That would be a bit of a career change!"

I laughed too. It sounded a bit strange now I had said it out loud. "No, I mean back when we were at school, silly."

He looked at me like I was mad. I realized I needed to tell him about my conversation with Sue and how I was going to fictionalize the book.

"I see," he said, after I'd told him all the character changes. "So what do you have in mind for me and Sue then?"

My cunning plan, I explained, was to make him a spaced-out pothead and drug dealer. His supplier would be my sister's scary and violent boyfriend. My sister would be extra bossy, overconfident and very popular. However, she would be having a secret, forbidden lesbian affair with one of the girls at boarding school. She would be accidentally discovered by Bug *in flagrante delicto* one afternoon and be terrified that he was about to expose her indiscretion. The joke would be that Bug was so out of it from smoking pot that he hadn't seen anything

"Well, that's quite a story transformation," he replied when I had finished, smiling so I knew he approved.

The next day, when Bug left to drive home, my fingers flew across the keyboard with renewed inspiration. Finally, finally, I was getting some work done.

But midway through the afternoon, the enormity of what I would have to do dawned on me. I stopped typing. It had taken so much time and effort to write the first three parts of my book, did I really think I could rewrite it all as a piece of fiction now? The energy drained out of me. I felt daunted by the task ahead. What would be my new persona? I was the main character, after all. Which of my many flaws would I exaggerate to comedic proportions? I would have to rewrite the entire book. All of it. Even my over-edited first chapter that was just about perfect. I sat. Minutes ticked by. Nothing. Like the sea mist creeping over the shore, I lost my creativity in a fog of indecision and my writer's block firmly established itself once more.

I finished off the last few hours of my precious retreat writing a post for my blog and wasting time on Facebook. On Monday I drove home dejected and disappointed that I was no further along than when I arrived.

Six months later I found myself still floundering with how to resolve my dilemma. And then a miracle happened. I was at a literary festival in San Francisco and met up with an editor whose online workshop I had taken a few months earlier and whose opinion I respected. When she asked me how my book was coming along, I explained my predicament.

"So what if there isn't any clear-cut reason why your sister and your husband don't like each other?" she said. "That often happens in real life. There aren't always nice, easy answers. Sometimes people don't like each other. Just say you don't know why and then you could 'perhaps-it'."

"Perhaps-it?" I asked.

"Yes, like . . . perhaps she was jealous, perhaps your husband fancied her, perhaps it was past-life karma, perhaps, perhaps, perhaps," she explained.

"Ooh, okay," I answered, as the penny dropped and I understood. And suddenly, a vast weight dropped off my shoulders and I could see the way forward. Sue didn't need to have closet gay tendencies; she could just be a loving, slightly overprotective big sister. Bug didn't have to be a drug dealer; he could remain his romantic over-the-top self, with a few bad habits. I could keep my book the way it was but just imagine some possible reasons why they didn't get on. It was so simple. I didn't have to rewrite the whole damn book. Why hadn't I thought of it earlier? I felt a huge sense of relief and the tiniest stirrings of excitement in my belly.

Now I just needed another writing retreat...

Claire Hennessy is also the author of the essay "The Reluctant Author."

Winging It
MJ Brodie

OUT OF THE BLUE, JUST A COUPLE OF MONTHS BEFORE my son was born, my husband received an interesting proposition from a company in California for which he had always wanted to work. It was his dream job. The only problem was that it was five thousand miles away from where we were, a small town in Scotland.

I had only ever been to the East Coast of the United States and while I, like nearly all Irish people, had various long-lost American cousins in New York and Chicago, I knew nobody in California. It seemed impossibly far away. The contract for my husband's new job arrived the day that our son was born. We were a little distracted that day, as you can imagine, probably too distracted to think straight. Later that night he called me at the hospital to say that he had signed the contract.

Visa stipulations meant that I would not be allowed to work or seek work in the United States for at least two years, possibly longer. What on earth was I going to do over there when I had been working, part-time or full-time, since I was seventeen? Certain more conservative factions of the family were pleased. It might have taken the entire might of the US government, they thought, but at last our daughter-in-law has seen the light and realized that children need their mother at home! Others worried that I would find myself very alone, however, isolated at home all day with a small baby in a foreign country and no family nearby. "With a baby?" they asked. "Won't you be lonely?"

I had no idea what they meant. Lonely? I would have my son, obviously. How could I be lonely with him by my side all the time? High on baby hormones, it had yet to hit home to me that it takes most human children two years or more to speak with any degree of coherence. I also underestimated just how hard it can be to make it out of the house with a baby and all his baby paraphernalia in tow. But I was sure we could make it work. Americans are more friendly after all, I told myself, not like us uptight Europeans.

As a distraction from more mundane practicalities of moving to a new country, I obsessed over finding the right stroller for my son that would be good on hot California days compared to our sturdy, heavily insulated Scottish pram, built to withstand gale force winds and driving rain, a bestseller in Russia. My stroller was all *Prime of Miss Jean Brodie* and in California I would clearly need something a little more Katy Perry. For some reason this frivolous concern took up a lot of my energy. The least of my worries was loneliness.

In truth, however, it did appall me a little to think of myself as a California housewife. Homemaker, as it said on my visa form. Homemaker. Ugh. My husband and I turned this awful slight on my person into a running joke. We laughed about our new life turning me into a Valium-addled zombie or the Mrs. Brown character in *The Hours,* crying in her Los Angeles kitchen over a cake that didn't turn out right, the palm trees and endless sunshine mocking her misery.

And so we moved and so I slid, oblivious and dazed, into life as a full-time parent, something I never thought I would be. And, yes, it was lonely, lonelier than I imagined. When you are a full-time parent to a tiny baby, it's easy to slip into isolation, tied to the home by a baby's endless naps and feeds and demands. Stay-at-home mothers are supposed to be "yummy mummies," or whatever the California equivalent of that should be, something even yummier no doubt. We are supposed to be out lunching all the time with friends while babies snooze peacefully in their strollers, or baby-jogging around the park clad head-to-toe in Lulu Lemon. The reality is a little different.

When we first moved over, we lived in San Francisco and, desperate to explore the city, I did the most I could to be adventurous with my son. I took him all around the city, up and down its vertiginous hills, in his sling or thoroughly researched slinky red stroller.

Little by little, however, life began to slow down. We moved to suburbia to be closer to my husband's job and my son's needs became more complex than getting milk and sleep on a regular basis. Once again, I found myself "leaning out," all the way to suburbia, for the sake of the men in my life.

In the suburbs, the daily routine of life as a full-time parent slowly began to grate on me. The strangest change for me was the long days without adult conversation, as my husband rarely got back home before eight at night and often traveled on business for weeks at a time.

My husband and I had met through talking, staying late to set the world to rights in a café in Berlin after what had originally been a brunch meet-up with mutual friends. We were still talking at one in the morning on the subway home. We both still love to carry conversations on late into the night but that is much harder to do when you have a baby waking you up at five the next morning. It is also harder to do on Face Time from Tokyo to California.

The other strange thing was how housebound I had become. They don't call it "housewife" for nothing. I was beginning to feel more married to our house than to my husband. I saw more of the house than I did of him and probably talked to it more as well, cursing its lack of air conditioning or awkward kitchen layout.

It didn't help that my son had started to develop a personality of his own around the same time. The little chap had always been so obliging before, happy to loll about in a sling or lie on a play mat for an hour as required. Now he had the temerity to start wanting to pursue his own interests, crawling about the house and trying to chew electrical cables and refusing to cooperate with my selfish need to read a book or sit in a café.

He also developed a disconcerting habit of issuing blood-curdling screams as soon as the wheel of his stroller would point in the direction of Peet's Coffee / Barnes & Noble / our favorite restaurant / any outpost of civilization where adults and the child-free congregate. It was as if he knew that he could stop me in my tracks with just one such scream, forcing me to back shamefaced out of many an establishment and head for home to allow the pint-sized tyrant to get on with his own interests. Whatever they might be.

This is the one of the dilemmas of full-time parenthood. Babies stop you from doing anything remotely interesting that you want to do but the blighters don't actually want to do anything themselves either, not anything interesting anyway. They want to roll around the floor, climb on shelves, break things, giggle, stare into space, talk gibberish and have their whims attended to like tiny, crazy emperors.

Taking care of a young baby, I felt that my days were strangely full and empty at the same time. I was on call for all of my son's pressing, irregular needs but in between that I had free time. Except that it was never free. I always felt as though I was waiting, stuck at some permanent bus stop, waiting for my son to wake up or finish his meal or cry out for my help or need a change and so it never felt as though my mind was my own.

It felt as though I was in solitary confinement for a crime I didn't commit with no reading materials or television and with a particularly cute chimpanzee as my jailor. Make that a drunken cute chimpanzee that keeps on falling over and hurting himself and having irrational outbursts of rage.

For me, used to my independence and life of the mind, it felt lonely and exhausting. The truth of Doris Lessing's words was suddenly brought home to me: *"There is nothing more boring for an intelligent woman than to spend endless amounts of time with small children."* This from a woman who abandoned her two young children in Africa to move to London and make it as a writer. She did win a Nobel Prize for literature so we can only hope that made it all worthwhile.

I loved being with my son and couldn't imagine leaving him for more than a few hours, much less a Doris Lessing scenario where I ran away to live a life of the mind. Still, I felt the need to do something to combat my isolation. So I turned, as I have at many difficult points in my life before, to writing. It started out as writing in a journal during nap times and in the evenings when my son was asleep. I told myself that the journal would be a nice record of my son's first year that I could keep forever.

With my husband away so often and my family five thousand miles away, there was no one I could talk to about my son's daily achievements, no one who was interested in the minutiae of mothering, and so it felt good to record it all, no matter how bad or good the writing. I wrote wondering whether it was a good idea to do baby-led weaning, whether my son was delayed in learning to crawl or whether it was normal to still be belly-crawling at eleven months, whether he had actually said "up" this morning or if I had imagined it, whether he was out of sorts today because he had a cold or if it was teething.

Unfortunately, my writing time often coincided with "wine time," and entries soon began to turn maudlin, focusing on my frustration at being home alone so much rather than the joys of watching my son grow and neat cataloguing of all his important milestones. After he had gone to sleep in the evening, after the usual bedtime battles, and before my husband came home, I would hammer out my frustration on our old MacBook, feeling sorry for myself.

Besides these more maudlin moments, however, I did also write about the good times to remind myself of how much I loved my time with my son in spite of all our ups and downs. I wrote about the look of awe and fascination on his face as we stood at our bedroom window to watch the tree surgeons come in their truck and crane to tend to the birch tree across from our house. I wrote about the first time we took my son to the beach and laughed as he ran fiercely towards the waves, determined to get soaked in the freezing Pacific brine. I wrote about the first time my son laid his head on my shoulder and said "Mama," making all the lonely days of our early months together worthwhile.

Writing like this was a way of getting my mind back to myself again. Instead of having my head full of schedules and naps and messes and tantrums and meal plans, I had time and space to clear my head and think about what I was experiencing. Children are very "in the moment" and young children especially flit from one whim to another. Writing was a way of creating permanence for me, something solid to hold onto, to make the memories last.

As part of my new adventures in writing, I revisited old journals and short stories that I had written in my early twenties and realized that all that youthful scribbling was actually good to read back on. It brought me back to a time of my life when everything seemed very confused and daunting, when I made some of the important decisions that were still affecting my life today. The short stories, which I had buried long ago in a shoebox and dismissed as juvenile ramblings, were actually still interesting to read and revealing of who I was at that time.

Inspired by how much I was enjoying writing again, I signed up for an online course in creative writing at Stanford University and encountered a supportive writing environment for the first time. I discovered Anne Lamott's concept of the "shitty first draft"—that all writers start somewhere and good writing is work, not something perfect that just spills out of your mind ready-formed. Instead of dreading deadlines as I had in my pre-child career, I suddenly found myself looking forward to our weekly writing exercises and thinking all day—in between songs and games and walks in the park—about what direction to take my writing in. The companionship of fellow students in my writing courses also gave me the confidence to realize that we all have worthwhile stories to tell, no matter what our personal circumstances are.

What surprised me most, however, was that writing actually helped me to be a better mother. Since I finally had something that I was doing for me, I no longer felt so frustrated with the routine day-to-day of parenting a toddler. More importantly, however, I no longer felt that loneliness was my enemy. Instead, I realized that being alone can foster creativity, forcing us to think deeper and be comfortable with ourselves. And being happy in your own company is a gift for anyone but especially for a writer.

So it turns out that life as a California housewife doesn't have to involve Valium and hysterical sobbing at the kitchen table, as my husband and I had joked about. Thankfully, writing is all the Valium I need and it is proving to be just as addictive a drug. The difference is that this is an addiction I never want to break.

MJ Brodie is a recent arrival to California from Ireland (via Germany, Belgium and Scotland) and has slowly adjusted to endless sunshine and positive thinking. She has always written and blogged and is now taking postgraduate courses in writing with Berkeley Extension and Stanford. A mother of one, she blogs on literature, politics and sometimes parenting at *A Fresh Eye* (suilnua.blogspot.com). You can follow her on Twitter @suilnua.

Filed Under "Writing"

Erin Erickson

I HAVE FANTASIES ABOUT BECOMING A MOVIE STAR OR even marrying one. I also have fantasies about writing a book and being an acclaimed author. Perhaps they are equally unlikely. So, to the relief of those who care about me and those who have observed my thespian skills, I have abandoned all efforts to become a movie star. But I have not abandoned my writing fantasy. In fact, it is that fantasy that drives me to pursue my passion for writing and feeds my minor addiction to writing retreats.

The idea of spending a weekend, or better yet a week, on an island with other writers just gives me a feeling that my life must be interesting. "She's one of those literary types," people might say. Or, "She's a writer and did you know she also plays the piano. Classical, with a special interest in the impressionist period." I would be worldly and respected for my knowledge of aesthetics. I might like my writing to be rooted in philosophy, so I could throw around words like "ontology" and "epistemology." I might even like to *be* a philosopher, just so I can understand the wisdom of ages that professorial types toss around as freely as children tossing a ball on the playground. But I am not a philosopher; I am a writer, though sometimes I doubt that as much as the former.

See, I do not actually write for pretense, to sound like a philosopher or an artist, or to be respected. I write to see if after telling my story any respect remains. I write to absolve myself of the judgment I feel for my shortcomings, as if putting it out in the world makes it all okay. I write to see if anyone will be left when I finish telling my story. I write to not be alone.

Sometimes I imagine my death. I imagine my family finding my folder, the one labeled, "writing," on the tab, printed of course with my label maker and neatly stored in a box with similarly labeled files. I imagine them reading my work and finally understanding. Maybe even feeling sorry for not seeing me as I really am while I was here. I imagine the papers spread out on a table with pictures of me with my children, while mourners walk by to take it in. "I had no idea," they might exclaim. "I'm so glad her mother found these." But then it sinks in, the sickness of this thought and the realization of what I am, in the end, really after. I just want to be seen, so I write because maybe someday someone will see me.

Erin Erickson is a specialist in maternal-child health and has extensive experience speaking on issues related to maternal-child health and parenting. She hosts a weekly podcast, *Mom Enough*™, which focuses on topics related to motherhood in today's world. In her life outside of work, she is pursuing a doctorate degree in nurse-midwifery. Erin lives in Minneapolis with her two children and, even though she is busy parenting and working, she manages to squeeze in time for writing, primarily by attending writing retreats.

Back in the Stirrups Again

Mindy Uhrlaub

IN MY NIGHTMARE, I LIE ON MY BACK, MY LEGS APART AND my feet in the stirrups, staring up at the cottage-cheese ceiling. The gynecologist sniffs from under the paper blanket and states, "This thing stinks."

I wake up screaming, only to realize that my dream is a metaphor for being rejected by the Squaw Valley Community of Writers. The cliché is so appropriate. If writing a novel is like gestating a baby, then having my novel critiqued by others is like the monthly OB visit.

Submitting my writing to Squaw was not the first time I had had creative works judged. For eight years, I played in a band. We were adored by many and detested by others. Yet I seldom felt the sting of rejection from music festivals, knowing that the next great opening slot was just around the corner. I briefly cried with band mates over bad record reviews, but then realized that maybe the vocals were mixed too hot, or the song order was off.

After music came film. I wrote, produced, and finally sold a feature that claimed almost ten of my post-college years. The crew and I knew it was a long shot when we applied for Sundance, and when the movie was rejected, everyone shrugged it off. The odds that any independent film gets into Sundance are pretty slim. When the movie was accepted for the Palm Beach International Film Festival, I reasoned that it was because of the strong soundtrack, brilliant camerawork, and great locations. I never took full credit for my film because it was a collaboration by so many people.

Sharing my writing with others is different. There is nobody to praise for it rocking or blame for it sucking besides me. I am completely exposed, unprotected under a thin paper blanket. Just like the monthly look-see when I was pregnant, I find myself alone, staring at the cottage-cheese ceiling again.

Of course, I know I am not completely alone. Right before I hit *send* on my submission to Squaw, my husband, Kirk, said, "Wait. Let's just go through the formatting one more time."

I realize that this was his way of holding my hand as the OB strapped the fetal heart-rate monitor on me. We went over the formatting again. Writing this novel has been a deeply personal and solitary journey for me, but Kirk has been with me the whole way. It's a story about an eleven-year-old African girl who is tortured and displaced by a militia group, but who survives in the jungle of a country that is the worst place in the world to be a girl. It's not a light book, Kirk says, but he's read it all. While I went through weeks of begging for paperwork to be notarized by the embassy at the Democratic Republic of the Congo for my research trip, he was busy untangling my visa application at Travel Document Services. When I got on the plane to Congo to visit hospitals and women's shelters, he was taking off a week of work to watch our sons, Ethan and Alex.

The kids are aware of the intensity my book demands. They know that sometimes their favorite snacks don't appear in the snack drawer in a timely manner. The eight hours of volunteer time at school each month have been cut to four, and they're okay with that because they know I have to finish my book. They always understood that I had a life outside of play dates and recorder lessons, but they never understood how important it was to me until I got that letter from Squaw.

There it was, plain as day. I held the letter in my hand and stood out on the front verandah and felt the sting of heat well up in my eyes. No, I thought. This is an exercise in grace and humility. You will not cry because it sends a bad message to the boys, I told myself. I walked into the kitchen. Kirk took one look at me and folded me in his arms.

"I'm so sorry, my Cute. I know how hard you tried," he consoled.

"It's okay," I whispered. Alex ran over, threw his arms around both of our knees and said, "Mommy, I love you no matter what."

What sweetness and light. And then Ethan came in from playing with the dog in the yard. I turned to him with my eyes brimming.

"No crying, Mom. You just have to try again. When I didn't make the Breakers team, did I stop playing soccer? No, I just did the rec league. You have to get up there and keep writing."

Jesus, I thought. Who taught them all of this? Could it be that all of those formative acceptances and rejections of my music and film days placed me in a better position to help my kids with the success and failure of their endeavors? The support network of my family feels so familiar, just like the collaboration between my crew members or band mates.

I always thought that my first rejection from a writer's conference would be an inoculation against future rejections. Or a way of learning how to be graceful when faced with acceptance or praise. But really, it has been an initiation into the world of sharing. Although giving my manuscript to others can make me feel vulnerable, I am never alone when my work is read by others. And when the rejection letters arrive, my family huddles around me. The next time I apply to a writer's conference, when the only thing between my nakedness and the cold exam room is a thin paper blanket, I will remember to be glad someone is holding my hand.

Mindy Uhrlaub graduated from the University of Denver with an MA in mass communications, while somehow still touring with her band, 40th Day. The group has opened for many bands including the Smashing Pumpkins and Kansas. She wrote her first feature film, *STALLED,* drawing on her experience touring with the band. She lives in Northern California with her husband Kirk (whom she met while shooting her film) and their two young sons. Her current project is a novel, *Unnatural Resources,* which chronicles the coming of age of a girl in the war-torn Democratic Republic of the Congo. The three men in Mindy's life are not thrilled about her traveling back and forth to research the Congo, but it beats touring with a band.

Shine, Shine, Shine

Steven Friedman

Shine, shine, shine. Yes, just let it shine.
—The Fresh Beat Band

DEAR MAYA AND MIGUEL,

About a half hour before Mommy died, ending her five-year battle with breast cancer, I clasped my hand into hers and told her that I would always love her. It was just before midnight.

Miguel, you were not quite a teenager at twelve and a half, and you weren't home, having chosen with my prodding to remain with your best friend, Chris, and his parents, for the weekend when I sensed Mommy might die soon. You'd told me you did not want to be home when Mommy died. I said I understood, and I did. You retreat inward during dark times and I know death upsets you. You once refused to let me finish reading *Old Yeller* when you found out the dog died in the end.

Maya, you were a few months shy of turning five, and were asleep upstairs in your own bed, which rested right near the custom-made California king-sized chest bed Mommy and I had bought just after Miguel was born, almost seven years after she and I got married on a typically fog-shrouded San Francisco day.

Miguel and Maya, this letter is part of the sharing I will always do to make sure you remember the woman who loved you so, so much. Whether it is the photo albums I compiled for each of you shortly after Mommy died or this letter or the stories I will always tell, I promise to help keep memories of Mommy alive for you.

Two days before Mommy died, after I squeezed three separate syringes filled with three different types of oral pain medication against the inside of her cheek, Mommy had slipped into a deep, deep sleep, not like the fairytale kind where a kiss would awaken her. My main job, I felt, was to help control Mommy's pain. There had been too many pain crises that had sent her to the hospital in the middle of the night and she'd started complaining that her legs were in a vise grip, so I was now administering what the hospice said were unbelievably large doses of methadone, morphine, and Ativan every two to three hours and four phenobarbital suppositories each day.

On the night she died, I held her hand in mine and knew our time together was short. I said, "Verna, when you are ready to go and join your mother in heaven you should go. She is waiting for you."

You might remember how Mommy did the same for Grandma Chela two years earlier as Grandma lay dying in a hospital in San Francisco. You were home with a sitter as Mommy and I, both her brothers and their spouses, Grandpa, and two of your cousins clustered around Grandma's bed in the ICU to help usher her to the next part of her soul's journey.

Grandma had been in the hospital for two weeks and comatose for those last three days, but Mommy's brothers hoped for a miracle. Mommy remained resolute and knew Grandma would never want to live on life support, her body kept afloat by artificial means, so Mommy urged everyone to accept the inevitable and say good-bye. By the time the doctor turned off the respirator and pulled out all the tubes and wires connecting Grandma to "life," it was only twenty minutes before Grandma took her last breaths.

Mommy never left Grandma's side that last day of Grandma's life, not even to use the bathroom. She constantly stroked her hair, gently caressed her cheeks and forehead with her hands and lips, and pressed moistened hand towels against Grandma's face to cool her.

Mommy and Grandma were so close. Mommy took Grandma to doctor's appointments and on vacation with us; and Miguel, after you were born, Grandma traveled an hour to our home by bus from San Francisco with a pot of chicken soup to help Mommy recover her strength.

I know how much Mommy loved Grandma. But their love was much different from the love between Mommy and me. I know I've told you that I proposed to Mommy after dating her for only seven weeks. When we first met we biked over the Golden Gate Bridge into Marin and sampled great meals and desserts in different San Francisco neighborhoods and talked about politics and the similar ways we saw the world, and joked and teased each other about everything from the simple lunches I made every day to her competitive side. I just had this magical, shivery feeling around and away from her. This woman who'd read more than 20 books to prepare for motherhood, always typed up to-do packing lists before vacations, organized our home and cooked most meals, rarely complained at work when tasks were heaped upon her, and always cuddled with you and me even up to a week before she died.

Shortly after Mommy's doctor sent her home from the hospital and told us to contact the hospice, Mommy decided to write cards to you. Birthday cards, holiday cards, graduation cards, even cards for each of you to share with a spouse should either or both of you ever marry. Mommy left you a written legacy, nuggets of sweetness, of herself, her voice that will be with you forever, which is another reason why I write this letter to you: I honor her memory by adding to her legacy.

Mommy was determined that each of you would have, at the very least, birthday cards from her until you were eighteen. She committed to write several cards each day. At first, it was easy. She would breeze through a card in her typically thoughtful way, reading and rereading each paragraph before she continued, sharing those early cards with me as tears rolled down my cheeks.

She used the Internet to research the years when she was ten, for example, or a teenager, and described what was happening in her world when she was the same age as you'd be celebrating when you read her cards. As the weeks progressed and the medicines clouded her mind at times, leaving her sleepy or confused or agitated, she still plowed on and wrote the cards.

One time I said to her, "Verna, I can be your secretary and you could dictate the cards to me."

"No," she insisted, "I have to write them myself. I want the kids to see what I went through."

Not because she needed you to know how much she was suffering or in pain, but how she struggled to write the cards herself as her gift to you. And I know when you read them and see her words and see the scribbles and cross-outs and mistakes, you will really feel your mother's devotion to you.

So, as I held Mommy's hand and nestled against her, I fell asleep for ten minutes with our apricot-colored miniature poodle, Gigi, on my stomach. Suddenly Gigi jumped off of me onto the floor, which woke me up. I looked over at Mommy and stroked her hair and lightly touched her face. Her breathing was more labored and her chest was heaving.

It was close to midnight, so I went to the kitchen to prepare her medications for the night, while Faye, who'd always been a patient and attentive caregiver and seemed to truly adore Mommy, sat by her side. As I was loading everything into various syringes, Faye said urgently, "Steve."

I bolted into the living room. "You didn't have to run," said Faye. Mommy's chest still heaved and the gaps between each breath were a few seconds. She was very pale. I knelt down almost diagonal to her chest and knew she was about to die.

"Faye, please go upstairs to the bedroom on the right, and wake up Jim and Liz," I said.

Mommy's brother, Uncle Jim and your Auntie Liz, rushed downstairs, and minutes later Mommy exhaled for the last time. We watched her chest rise and fall, rise and fall, and then stop. She was gone. I buried my head in her left arm and cried. Jim and Liz, each seated above her head, cried. Faye sat quietly, a stunned look stretched across her face.

I felt numb. I'd known the day was coming with intellectual awareness (and certainty), but when death entered the room my entire world was thrown off balance. My best friend and lover had died, and even though I knew it was coming soon, I still trembled inside and wondered if I was part of some cruel joke or nightmare.

And I felt empty because I knew Mommy was gone and I knew that our plans and dreams for the future with you and with each other had been tragically altered, terminated. We'd said goodbye to Mommy officially a week earlier, in a session guided by a hospice social worker and a therapist, but that was mainly for you two.

Mommy and I had already shared our last goodbyes and talked about our deeper feelings and fears over the last several weeks of her life. We'd spoken about finances and what would happen to you if I were to die; we talked about our love for each other and how much we'd miss each other, not grow old together and travel by car and bike across the globe. So the gathering that day, initiated by Mommy, was so she could in a fairly unaltered and lucid state tell you how much she was going to miss you, miss seeing you grow up and become wonderful people.

Maya, you alternated between lying near Mommy on the hospital bed downstairs and flitting about upstairs with the therapist, who specialized in working with younger children. Miguel, you sat by Mommy's side and cried as you talked about being a teenager without a mother. Mommy reminded you to always be good and find passions to pursue in life.

Four hours after Mommy died, I finally dozed off in the bed upstairs, but heard you, Maya, rustling three hours later in your princess bed near ours, around 7:00 a.m. You opened your eyes and smiled at me. I pulled you, wisps of brown hair across your face, into bed with me. I was still numb and I was exhausted, and I was about to tell you, the sweetest girl in the world, that your best, best friend and mommy had died seven hours before. I should've just let out a primal scream.

"Maya," I started, quietly instead, "Mommy is now a star in heaven." This was something we'd been saying to you both since Mommy and I had read Liplap's Wish and been drawn to the sweet and tangible way the author had explained death and grieving. "She is with Grandma Chela."

"No," you said, "you're joking."

"No, she died," I said. "But she's a star in heaven and will always be in our hearts."

"I'm going to check downstairs," you said. I wanted to cry, scream, shout, pound my fists on the floor or wall, but I felt I had to stay in control for you. And maybe for myself, too. I might have feared completely losing it if I'd let go.

But the hospital bed had already been stripped clean of its sheets and air mattress. All that was left was a bare frame. Mommy's body had been quietly removed hours earlier in the darkness of the early morning. You came back moments later. My heart broke yet again when I saw your face and I knew what you had just learned with utter and irrevocable certainty.

"Oh, I am sad," you said. "Mommy died." Then you looked at me and said words I will never, ever forget, "Don't worry, Daddy, I'll take care of you."

I held you tightly. How could it be that you'd lost the woman who'd filled Disney Princess sticker books with you, had walked with you for hours and hours at Disneyland after the cancer had returned because she wanted to give you the ultimate Princess experience, the woman who read you bedtime stories, and snuggled in bed with you, and hugged you, even after her cancer had filled her spine, pelvis, sternum, and liver and had practically immobilized her and left her in a constant state of pain? And I thought, "Maya, you are such a gift."

The morning was a blur. Maya, you nibbled on breakfast, and said you absolutely did not want to go to preschool. You cried. "But," you added, "can I still have my play date with Annika?" I made plans to drop you off outside the preschool so you could stay with Annika's mother, Torhalla, until school ended and then you would play with Annika for most of the day. Just as I had promised Miguel that his immediate world—play dates, sports, school, other extracurricular activities and outings—would not change much after Mommy's initial cancer diagnosis in 2006, I wanted your normal day-to-day existence, Maya, to remain the same. One of the things Mommy and I had read in one of those "When a Parent Has Cancer" books is that maintaining a routine for children is vitally comforting and reassuring.

I rushed back from the preschool parking lot because Amanda, one of my best friends and someone who adored Mommy like a sister, was on her way over. As I got home, the phone rang. It was another friend, Mercedes, calling to check in.

"How are things going?" she asked.

"Well, actually, Verna died earlier this morning . . . "

"Oh, Steve, I am so sorry," she said. "I was just calling on my way to work." Mercedes re-routed herself to our house and joined Amanda, who had just arrived, and me on the kitchen floor, where the two of them sat with me for hours.

I told them how Mommy didn't really like me when we first met and I'd thought she was aloof, about our first date to a Wynton Marsalis concert in San Francisco and how Mommy wore a black leather miniskirt when she arrived at my house for a homemade dinner—Swiss chard frittata. I described her joy at becoming a mother, our vacations to Israel, Mexico (twice), how her sometimes painfully shy side often hid her humor and her deep intelligence. I talked about her passions for fitness and dance, how her dance team had even placed first one year at Carnaval in San Francisco's Mission District. And even though they already knew all of this, I described how she was a great friend to many and an even more wonderful mother.

After Amanda and Mercedes left to give me time alone and to get ready for the rest of the day, I hopped on the Life Cycle for thirty minutes for a much needed session of sweat, which, as you know, I cling to daily as a fitness addict. That day I was numb and scared and elated to elevate my heart rate and happy to escape for a brief time my sadness and grief. Pedaling was an out-of-body experience. I felt comforted by the routine but completely out of it as the reality of Mommy's death sank in more deeply.

I showered and then drove to pick you up, Miguel, our lithe, brown-haired son. I was waiting for you on the sidewalk near Miller Creek Middle School as you strolled up munching a Ben and Jerry's bar, huge flecks of chocolate spilling to the ground. I put my arm around you.

"Hey, Miguel," I blurted out as if I had to rush my words because I was so nervous, my voice wavering, tears clouding my eyes, "Mommy died this morning just after midnight. I think she was at peace. She just stopped breathing."

"You were there?"

"Yes," I answered.

You looked at me, sadness in your eyes, but you revealed no other emotion. I wanted to hold you, soak you up, but I also knew you needed some space, some distance, especially in front of your teenaged peers, where parental displays of affection are nearly outlawed. When you didn't say anything else, I offered that it was certainly fine for you to spend more time with Chris and his family. I also repeated how much Mommy loved you and that I knew how much you loved her. "Just make sure you tell me what you need," I added.

You ended up spending another week with the Allens, including three days in Tahoe over Labor Day weekend. By the time I retrieved you I was more than ready for what remained of our family to be reunited and together. I'd missed you terribly and I needed us to be together so I could hold onto both of you now more than ever, but I was glad you'd had the chance to have fun before returning to a home without Mommy.

Maya, that day Mommy died, you trudged up the front steps of our home after 7:00 p.m., exhausted and very sad, after your afternoon play date with Annika and her older sister.

You hadn't eaten any dinner, but you did remember some delectable treats someone had brought over a day or so ago. So after I broke several self-imposed parenting rules that deal with food, I allowed you to eat a comfort-food dinner of two cupcakes. Then we went outside and looked at the night sky.

"Tell me which star is Mommy," I said.

You pointed to a bright one that was twinkling right above our home. "That's Mommy," I said. "And look how she's smiling down on us."

"We can go out every night and look at Mommy," Maya said.

I gazed at the shining star and said, "I love you, Verna." Tears clouded my eyes and my voice shook. We'd pointed out stars before for my Grandmother Ida and for Marie's dog, and Mommy and I had talked about heaven and death with Miguel, but I never imagined that one day we'd be pointing to Mommy in the night sky, a shiny orb in a river of blue-black darkness.

"I love you, Mommy," Maya said. And I somehow felt the sadness and longing in your voice, as I again confronted how surreal it was to communicate with someone we loved so, so much, but who was now beyond our physical reach. And how strange and scary, down to my very core, it felt to feel so alone and anxious about being the sole parent to our children. I felt lost without Mommy and her logic and planning and organization. I felt almost dizzy as I realized that Mommy had been ripped away from us, from you, from me. I knew I could and would manage without Mommy, but I didn't want to. She and I had been a team and she had been a perfect complement to my gregarious and neurotic nature.

Mommy was quiet, yes, but she was silly and made up silly songs for both of you when you were babies, and pushed you in carriages for long walks when you were babies to Starbuck's, the park, the library. And she also loved horror movies and bathroom humor and preparing elaborate recipes that she followed exactly.

Mommy died while you, Maya, were asleep, and you, Miguel, were away. I truly believe she *chose* to die at a moment that would cause you the least disruption, pain, and trauma.

Maya, that night you and I stared up at the sky and you said again, "I love you, Mommy. I love you forever."

So I write these memories of Mommy's life and death for you both in order to make sure she is forever in your hearts and minds. And remember always: Mommy and I love you both forever and ever.

Love,
Dad

Steven Friedman is also the author of the essay "Not Afraid of Words."

The Story Behind
the Stories

ONCE UPON A TIME, A GROUP OF WRITERS WHO ALSO
happened to be parents attended monthly salons organized by a
San Francisco Bay Area bookstore. They wrote, gave each other
feedback, and, of course, chatted. The bookstore also scheduled
speakers, usually mothers who were authors or worked in publishing. Some of them went on to land their own book deals.

Then suddenly—quite suddenly, it seemed—the bookstore informed them that it had booked a children's literature
hour during their time slot. They were stranded. And ticked
off. They needed their fix. At the final salon the question arose:
Could they organize something like this for themselves? Meet,
write, listen to other writers?

"We'll meet the second Sunday of the month, like always,"
said Laurel Hilton ("Of Rats and Deadlines").

So, the very next month we met in a café in a little town
north of San Francisco, a dozen of us with our laptops and cal-
endars, notebooks, and a Melissa & Doug whiteboard that one
of the moms had borrowed from her preschooler (who sat and
colored quietly while munching on a bagel).

The meeting unfolded like the folktale *Stone Soup.* Marianne
Lonsdale ("Giving Birth to Creativity") took notes. Mary Allison
Tierney ("The Gingerdread Man") wrote ideas on the whiteboard.

"I can scout future locations," said one mom.

"I can help you," said another.

"I have marketing experience," chimed in a third.

Claire Hennessy ("The Reluctant Author," "Writer's Block Retreat") volunteered to start a blog and collect essays. Janine Kovac ("The Next Prompt," "Shut Up, Shelly") said she'd ask her writing teacher to be the guest speaker for the next meeting.

The following month we met at a dimly lit recreational center with creaky folding chairs. One writer brought strawberries. Another brought crackers. Our wine-country connection, Teri Stevens ("There Was a Before") brought a bottle of red and a bottle of white. A cup for donations to cover the rental space was put on the table next to the wine and crackers. Cary Tennis, writing teacher, workshop leader and advice columnist for Salon.com's "Since You Asked" was our first speaker. He brought his guitar and opened with a song about checking your ego at the door. He talked about his journey as a writer and shared Pat Schneider's "Five Essential Affirmations" from her book *Writing Alone and With Others.*

"One: Everyone has a strong, unique voice," he began, as we scratched away on notebooks and typed on laptops.

"Two: Everyone is born with creative genius.

"Three: Writing as an art form belongs to all people, regardless of economic class or educational level.

"Four: The teaching of craft can be done without damage to a writer's original voice or artistic self-esteem.

"Five: A writer is someone who writes."

We left energized and recharged. In the months to come we would meet at a cabin, a library, and in the living room of one of our members (Lorrie Goldin, "From Conception to the Empty Nest") before we found a home at the O'Hanlon Center for the Arts in Mill Valley.

Today we call ourselves the Write On Mamas. We have over 40 members who are based in the Bay Area and eight satellite members who live in Oregon, Minnesota, Maryland, and Calgary.

For most of us, family and kids are why we write. But they are also why we don't write. So that's our common ground. It's inspiring to come to a meeting and see a group of writers and know that they probably had the same struggle getting out the door or they're dealing with the same sticky situations that happen when you write about your family.

Our first group project was a reading for Lit Crawl, a pub crawl of literary readings that occurs on the last day of San Francisco's nine-day literary festival Litquake. In an upscale boutique in San Francisco's Mission District we read our essays on the theme "Your Mom Had Sex." The provocatively titled evening drew an audience of ninety to hear readings about a penis fashioned during macramé class (by a middle schooler, who else?), a mom's creative solution to her midday sexual fantasies, and the sorts of stories filed under "the things children ask" (such as the question put to our resident dad by his son, "Which is better, anal sex or oral sex?").

Our subsequent group projects have been less risqué: such as an A-Z Blog-a-thon in which we divvied up the alphabet into twenty-six blog posts written by twenty-six different Write On Mamas, and other readings in the Bay Area. *Mamas Write* is our first group-project-in-print.

We didn't set out to write an anthology, but everyone was writing some kind of story. Laurel Hilton wrote about her Ukrainian grandmother, the matriarch of her family, racing against the clock that was her grandmother's dementia. Dorothy O'Donnell ("A Label She Loves") wrote about her daughter who had been diagnosed with early-onset bipolar disorder. Steven Friedman ("Not Afraid of Words," "Shine, Shine, Shine") wrote to preserve the memory of his late wife. Mindy Uhrlaub ("Back in the Stirrups Again") wrote because she'd read a book (*King Leopold's Ghost*) and she couldn't get the Congo out of her mind. After reading every book about the Congo, she visited escorted by Human Rights Watch. A Congolese girl told her, "You'll just cry your white person's tears and go home." Instead Mindy started a novel about the Congo.

We wondered, What would it be like to read these stories in a collection? Some of us had published; some of us were just journalers; yet there was much overlap in our writing struggles and our process. Somehow too, there was a spark, a driving force that led us to this community, a nagging voice that kept us writing.

We started with a question: "Why do you write?"

Mamas Answer

*The Write On Mamas offer thoughts
and tips on writing*

How do you make time for writing or prioritize it?

LAUREL HILTON: I don't. It just happens when I have an obsession to explore an idea I am curious about . . . [I] grab a notebook
and write furiously in it.

JENNIFER VAN SANTVOORD: Prioritizing writing is something I
really struggle with. There always seems to be something more
pressing than sitting down to write. Because I don't write for
money (yet!) it's sometimes hard to stay motivated and to write
just for the sake of writing, when there are bills to pay, rooms
to clean, and dinners to cook.

JESSICA O'DWYER: I'm always ready to jot thoughts or observa-
tions or snippets of conversations in a notebook or on the back
of an envelope or scrap of receipt. This can happen any time or
anywhere. But for a sustained project, I must make a schedule—
"Drop off kids, go for walk, eat breakfast. Write." For more than
twenty years, I worked in offices where bosses expected me to
show up on time and get my job done, regardless of my mood or
level of inspiration. I try to bring that discipline to writing. Soon

enough, the clock strikes 2:30 p.m. for school pickup and my writing day is over. I remind myself: *You get to do this. So many people don't.*

beth touchette: I need help in prioritizing writing. I become grumpy if I don't make the time.

susan knecht: I schedule an hour in the morning when my son is at school and I don't have any work commitments. Usually reading something or watching a film sparks an idea that I've been tossing around and I relate it back to the novel—kind of like an extra puzzle piece that needs integration into the whole of the story.

mindy uhrlaub: Once the kids are at school, only the barking puppy and lunch get me out of the chair.

mary allison tierney: I prioritize my writing as follows: Get the kid to school (think about writing), exercise (think about writing), errands (think about writing), walk the dog (think about writing), empty dishwasher/swap laundry loads (think about writing), eat something (watch recorded *Daily Show/Colbert Report*), answer emails/texts-update calendar (think about writing), take kid from school to music/sports/arts thing (think about writing), make dinner (think about writing), pour glass of wine/supervise homework/load dishwasher (think about writing), brush and floss (think about writing), sit down at my desk and nod off. Some days are better than others . . .

marianne lonsdale: I have to schedule it on my calendar and even then I often don't follow the plan. My best writing happens in the café at my gym on Saturday mornings after I work out, or if I get out of town for a weekend. Finding time is always an issue.

LORRIE GOLDIN: I usually have too much time on my hands, and although this sounds like an enviable luxury, it is not. My worst writing days are when I have a long stretch of time. I do better with short intervals and stolen moments.

ERIN ERICKSON: I find it difficult to carve out the time and space to write. With two kids and the typical full calendar of today's family, the only way I manage to write is to go on writing retreats. There's something great about sitting in a big cozy chair by a fireplace with one task at hand—writing. When I am away at a cabin, I can let go of my worries, forget about the stack of laundry on the kitchen table, and pretend for a moment that my only responsibility is to myself and my words.

What helps you write?

MEGHEN KURTZIG: My Fitbit. I set the silent alarm for 5:15 a.m. and get in an hour of writing before the family wakes up. (Thanks to Write On Mamas guest speaker Christine Carter for the suggestion.) I have a writing-specific calendar so that I hold myself accountable for what I want to accomplish and I can see it on a timeline. I also take advantage of long plane and car rides.

LORRIE GOLDIN: Recently I had an epiphany that it's not so much writing that's a torture, but the avoidance of writing. Deadlines and themed calls for submissions help. Being on track with my eating keeps me on track with my writing, and vice versa. With both of these endeavors, I ask myself what do I truly want and where will self-sabotage get me? I also like and sometimes even write morning pages—which I call toilet pages because that's where I write them and the venue pretty much sums up the quality of the writing.

PAMELA ALMA WEYMOUTH: Deadlines, frustration, the book-deal-dream, madness, self-flagellation help me write.

JANINE KOVAC: It always helps me to be around other people, even if it's just in a café. I'm less likely to procrastinate. That said, it also depends on what I'm writing. I rely on my Tuesday group (we meet on Wednesdays now) to help me write the hard stuff, which often comes out as a big jumble. But when I'm in the middle of something, the momentum comes from the writing itself. I'll write on the subway, in the car, before going to bed.

MARIA DUDLEY: Deadlines help me write. If I have a specific project and deadline, that will keep me in the chair. I also write in front of my students. The quality isn't always the best, but at least I am writing!

SUE LEBRETON: I take classes, mostly online. The deadlines keep me motivated and I can say with truth, "Mommy needs to do her homework." Plus the writing is fun and grounds me in the rest of my life. I am happier and everyone is happier when I am writing.

CLAIRE HENNESSY: The Write On Mamas help me write. Deadlines help me write. Passion to finish my book helps keep me in the chair. In 2014, I have prioritized writing by reducing my work week to four days — the fifth day is going to be my writing day.

Where do you write?

CYNTHIA LEHEW-NEHRBASS: I will write while getting my hair colored. The forty-five-minute processing time is awesome! My colorist likes to read my stories too. I've written while in the bathtub (even typing sometimes on my computer—trying not to get it wet— don't recommend this one)—but really, bath time for awhile was my only *me* time! And yes, I admit I've written on the toilet in the bathroom in the middle of the night to not wake my family.

STEVEN FRIEDMAN: I usually write at night after my kids are asleep, which is often past nine o'clock as my oldest is almost sixteen. One Saturday I wrote while my son was busy and my seven-year-old daughter was at a friend's house for a play date. I must admit that I will sometimes write for a few thirty-minute intervals at work—like right now.

MARY ALLISON TIERNEY: I write at the desk I set up in my son's abandoned bedroom, now that he's in college. It's convenient because it's across the hall from my thirteen-year-old daughter's room and I can keep an eye (sort of) on her laptop screen.

MJ BRODIE: One time I wrote up an idea I had while I was at the park with my son, keeping one eye on him while typing into the notes app on my phone.

BETH TOUCHETTE: I like to write on my desktop computer. I prefer a full-sized keyboard over that of a laptop. Writing on my desktop means I get to share the room with my teenage son and husband, which makes it hard to concentrate. I keep a little notebook in my purse. I've written some great stuff while waiting at the DMV and at the doctor's office.

JANINE KOVAC: A lot of my writing is born in Mary Hill's living room where we've been meeting every week for over two years. (Although sometimes we do change living rooms.) However, right now I am typing in my car waiting for my daughter to get out of school.

JOANNE HARTMAN: I often write using the voice app on my phone waiting in the carpool line at school, while stuck in traffic, and parked at the dog park (even when my dog is barking incessantly.) Which means the words, "Bad Dog" show up several times in what gets transcribed.

What holds you back from writing?

JENNIFER VAN SANTVOORD: Everything. Life. Kids. "To-do" lists. And unfortunately I often allow all this "stuff" to aid and abet in my writing procrastination.

STEVEN FRIEDMAN: Myself, my fears, my laziness.

MARIA DUDLEY: Lack of time holds me back from writing more. Also, I am an avid reader, and when I can't produce the kind of writing that I am reading, I get frustrated. It takes time to write something that I am proud of.

JANINE KOVAC: When I feel like I'm being pulled in a bunch of different directions, it's hard to focus on writing. These different forces can be family-related (have to drop off kids at school, clean the house, do the laundry, review notes for a meeting, go to yoga) or writing-related (I have a blog post to write! I have an outline to work on! I have to get that essay polished! I have to read that post by so-and-so).

JESSICA O'DWYER: The responsibilities of life hold me back. The ten thousand details that must be attended to today, now. That, and the fear I have nothing worthwhile to say.

SUSAN KNECHT: Not enough time! Having to work and make money, at times feeling tired from running the working mommy marathon.

CYNTHIA LEHEW-NEHRBASS: Fatigue. Chronic illness. Family demands. Getting caught up in the chaos of life. That little inner critic that likes to take down my creative nature with doubt and a desire for perfection.

MJ BRODIE: My son. (Ha! No, I can't really blame him.) Often it's fear of failure on my behalf. Sometimes I read over what I've written the day before and feel too discouraged to start hitting the keyboard again. So, negative self-talk often holds me back. I'm my own harshest critic!

CLAIRE HENNESSY: Writer's block. When I haven't written for ages, it seems like too daunting a task to get my head back into the space to continue with my memoir. Sometimes I have to spend a good hour or so rereading past chapters to get back into the flow and emotional state to continue writing properly.

MARIANNE LONSDALE: I get held back when I think my writing sucks or I don't know where my novel is going or I decide it's important to go grocery shopping instead.

LORRIE GOLDIN: Self-doubt, fear of exposure, guilt about wanting exposure, laziness, feelings of futility, imagining how much easier life would be if I just spent my free time gardening or reading or watching TV, imagining how much everyone hates me whenever I send out a Brag E mail. I feel repulsed by the amount of self-promotion involved in establishing "platform." Plummeting from the high of a brilliant first draft to rereading it and realizing it's terrible. The fear that once I get going, I won't ever want to come back to my normal life; I'll abandon my husband, children, work, and any notion of getting dinner on the table.

Do you have a favorite writing book?

MEGHEN KURTZIG: I'm currently working through *The Plot Whisperer* book and workbook. I am finding it incredibly helpful. (Thank you Write On Mama Cynthia Ash for the suggestion.)

STEVEN FRIEDMAN: I love writing books by Anne Lamott, Stephen King, and Dani Shapiro.

LORRIE GOLDIN: I don't read many writing books, though I have a pile on my night table whose wisdom I hope to procure through osmosis. I enjoyed Anne Lamott's *Bird By Bird* and *The Artist's Way* by Julia Cameron. My friend Jessica just raved about Dani Shapiro's *Still Writing,* and I have added it to my wish list.

MARIA DUDLEY: My favorite writing books are ones for children and teens, but they can help adults to be better writers, too. The best are *In the Middle* and *Lessons that Change Writers* by Nancie Atwell and *The Art of Teaching Writing* and *Units of Study* by Lucy Calkins.

SUE LEBRETON: Several books: Kate Hopper's *Use Your Words*; Beth Kephart's *Handling the Truth*; Stephen King's *On Writing*; Christina Katz's *Writer Mama* and *The Writer's Workout*.

JESSICA O'DWYER: Adair Lara's *Naked, Drunk, and Writing*, for its straightforward presentation and emphasis on finding the narrative arc. Dani Shapiro's *Still Writing*, for its eloquent reminder to listen, be quiet, and stay still.

CYNTHIA LEHEW-NEHRBASS: Francine Prose: *Reading Like a Writer*; Kate Hopper: *Use Your Words*; Anne Lamott: *Bird By Bird*; Betsy Lerner: *The Forest for the Trees*.

LAUREL HILTON: Stephen King's *On Writing* is *the* best writing book I've ever read. It keeps me inspired and coming back for more.

Writing retreats or classes you'd recommend?

MINDY UHRLAUB: Renting a house for a weekend with a writing friend works wonders!

LORRIE GOLDIN: I have gotten a lot out of Joyce Maynard's classes, particularly her intensive one-day workshop; Laura Deutsch and Leslie Keenan have also helped. I have also experienced massive writer's block after taking classes, so part of me just thinks I should listen to my significant writer's block after attending writing classes, and am considering listening to my husband, who says, "Why not just write instead of spending money and time going to classes?"

MARY ALLISON TIERNEY: Cary Tennis. My anthology piece "The Gingerdread Man" was born in the workshop he held for the Write On Mamas.

JANINE KOVAC: I love getaway writing retreats. I never get as much writing done as I hope to, but I have a different focus away from family and familial obligations and I'll find myself months later channeling that focus when I'm trying to write in my "normal" life. My favorite retreat is Kate Hopper's Faith's Lodge retreat in the middle of Wisconsin snow.

PAMELA ALMA WEYMOUTH: Pam Houston's Tomales Bay Writing Conference: Writing by Writers.

JESSICA O'DWYER: A paradigm shift occurred when I attended the Squaw Valley conference. Simply to be in the same room with a hundred-plus serious and focused writers showed me what could be possible if I worked hard. Honestly, though, every class I've taken—whether through a bookstore, continuing education, or with any of the outstanding writers based in the Bay Area—has taught me something.

STEVEN FRIEDMAN: Bob Welch's Beachside Writers Workshops are great.

MJ BRODIE: I just finished a great class in humor writing with Stanford Continuing Studies. It helped me to loosen up my funny bone and relax more about trying new strategies for writing.

LAUREL HILTON: I'm signed up to take a seminar sponsored by the Op-Ed Project, a social venture founded to increase the range of voices and ideas we hear in the world. (They hold workshops in major media markets throughout the United States.) This is a significant resource for me and I look forward to a dynamic exchange of ideas with fellow writers, journalists and editors. Thanks to Write On Mamas guest speaker Christine Bronstein for telling us about its existence!

MARY HILL: I definitely recommend Kate Hopper's online classes and her February Faith's Lodge retreat is my annual must-do. The cozy setting, Kate's brilliant direction and the community of writers all help me stretch. I find that my brain and body shift toward that writing space starting in early January, and that I always have a big breakthrough on the retreat or after.

What's the biggest surprise you've had in your writing or as a result of your writing?

JESSICA O'DWYER: How deeply fulfilled I feel by writing. And how consistent the process is: The piece must be bad before it can be good.

SUE LEBRETON: That my writing fills me with joy even if the topic is sad or dark.

JENNIFER VAN SANTVOORD: That it made me feel like a more

whole and complete person. Like what I had to say mattered to someone other than a toddler and a kindergartener.

MEGHEN KURTZIG: That I would love it. I was planning to use writing as a tool in my community health career but found that I love writing as much as [I love] health care.

CYNTHIA LEHEW-NEHRBASS: One of the biggest "aha" moments came when I did my first public reading of an emotional essay about my daughter. I initially was terrified in the process of sharing. But as I was witnessed in my moment of personal reveal, I did not crumble—I felt upheld and empowered. At the end, a woman stood up and applauded. She said later that she identified with my story. I learned that my memoir writing was not merely a "just for me" self-expressive tool to hide in a journal—it needed to be seen/read in the light of day.

BETH TOUCHETTE: The biggest surprise I have had with my writing was when my fifteen-year-old looked up the four KQED Perspectives I wrote (on his own) and complimented me.

MARIANNE LONSDALE: I had such low expectations of myself and my writing—there are so many things that have surprised me which might be small successes for someone else but are huge for me. For example, being accepted at the Squaw Valley Community of Writers Conference, being published anywhere and probably the biggest surprise is my willingness to call myself a writer.

MARY ALLISON TIERNEY: The biggest surprise I've had is that if

I write something down it won't kill me. Even the really yucky stuff. I can write it and get over it easier.

LORRIE GOLDIN: I wrote a piece called "Are We There Yet?" about my evolving views on gay marriage and the interplay between the law and social change. I really liked the piece and was forever changing the lead to keep it topical as the news changed, but I could never get it published. It ended up as a post on an obscure writing group's blog, where I imagined about eight dedicated members read it. Months later I got an email from a gay father who had somehow come across it and wrote to thank me for writing it. This was when the battle for and against Prop 8 raged through California. He wrote me about how the planes flying overhead with banners denouncing gay marriage traumatized his eight-year-old daughter, who had never before encountered any hatred of her family. He said that maybe my essay would change a mind or two, an inch at a time. I was surprised that my writing could find its way from obscurity into this man's life, and that he took the time to reach out to me. I was surprised that my writing mattered. I'm still surprised by how much this feeling alone keeps me going.

SUE LEBRETON: I think we are being great role models to our children when they see us following our passions and even when they do not seem to be paying attention, they are. The other day my son walked by and my computer was open. He glanced at it and said, "Oh, that's one of your old articles." Sure enough it was one I was tweaking to resubmit.

Acknowledgments

IF THERE'S ONE THING WE'VE LEARNED IN THE TWO YEARS it took to write, compile, and edit the essays for *Mamas Write,* it's that everything is more interesting if you tell it as a story. Thank you to Kate Hopper for dispensing this invaluable piece of advice as you gently and expertly edited our initial drafts over email correspondence and through your *Motherhood & Words* course. (And, when we were lucky enough to see you in person, over a glass of wine.) You helped us shape our inklings of ideas and focus our stories. It was such a pleasure to work with you.

Something else we learned about telling stories—they have to take place somewhere. Thank you to the O'Hanlon Center for the Arts, our monthly meeting spot. We couldn't imagine a more peaceful and cozy writing place complete with plenty of pillows and plenty of electrical outlets (a must for any writers' group), all in a setting graced by deer and redwood trees. Thank you to Blair Campbell of O'Hanlon for making us feel welcome and to Megan Wilkinson who confirms that yes, we did remember to reserve our space for the month.

The other setting for our stories is Bittersweet Café in Oakland (which specializes in hot chocolate and other chocolate delights). It turns out that chocolate is an excellent accompaniment to the toils of editing. More importantly, it's a powerful motivator when you need to schedule meetings.

Thank you, Penny and Diana for your smiles, your chocolate, and your sunny tables.

Stories have characters, too—such as the aforementioned kind and wise Kate Hopper, who prompted us to dig deeper and write more. Cary Tennis, whose keen eyes and easy manner made you a natural choice when we needed to take the next step for our group—it feels so fitting that you would be our first guest speaker, lead our first writing workshop, and then copy edit our first book. Norma Tennis, your graphic-design talents, attention to detail, and extensive knowledge of all things in e-formats and on iDevices have brought our book into the twenty-first century. To our behind-the-scenes team—thank you for helping us realize our vision.

Thank you to all our past speakers of the Write On Mamas who took time out of their busy lives to spend a Sunday afternoon with us: Carol Pott of Editorial Girl, author and editor Rachel Sarah, Christine Carter of Raising Happiness, übereditor Anika Streitfeld, blogger and author Samantha Schoech, Brooke Warner from She Writes, Robin Ekiss from Litquake, Linda Lee from AskMePC, Christine Bronstein from A Band of Women, Janis Cooke Newman from the Grotto and Lit Camp, and Caroline Grant of *Literary Mama* and the Sustainable Arts Foundation. You remind us how we are in full control of our effort but not the result, how our words affect others and how Facebook can be your friend if you're trying to build your platform, but when you're writing—not so much. You are inspirations to all of us.

And finally, thank you to our friends, families, and fellow writers who believed in our project and demonstrated support through extraordinary generosity.

They say it takes a village to raise a child. Turns out it also takes a collection of villages if that child has a parent with a passion to write. Thank you to our friends, family, and fellow writers who believed in our project and demonstrated support through their extraordinary generosity: Nina Abnee, Domini Anne, Sofia Larkin Appleby, Cindy Ash, Cindy Bailey, Barbara Ball, Lisa Barnett, Jinny Barrish, Suzi Banks Baum, Keith Benson, Claire Bindeman, Elroy and Phoebe Bode, Lisa Brussell, the Kramer Bryans, Marian Bryan, Cathy Burke, Dani Burlison, Nara Caliguri, Chloë Delafield, Karen Dixon, Nathalie Fraise, Ellen Gumbiner, Suzanne Helbig, Deborah Huber, Dixie James, Elvinia Johnson, Amy Kahn, Louise Keshaviah, Sharon Kovac, Rita Kovac, Janel Larson, Milinda Lommer, Amy London, Li Lovett, Celeste Low, Fionnuala McEvoy-Pecko, Dr. Alex Espinoza, Beth Mirsky, Jolene Munson, the Munson Family, Caitlin Myer, Maria Northcutt, Cindy Reynolds, Julia Ann Richards, Jessica Rider, Ranah Salih, Cleo Salisbury, Marty Van Santvoord, Hallie Sawyer, Greg and Greta Schoenberg, May Sheppard-Ketchner, Jillian Smith, G. Jeanne Stevens, Tina Stevens, Don and Norma Svet, Rosemary Taylor, Kara Thom, Paul Tomita, Andrea Torres, Mihail Varbanor, Morrie Warshawski, Shirley Williams, Michelle Woodward, Alene Wright, Eve Zamora, and Cathy Zwaska. This book is for you.

With our deepest gratitude,
Janine Kovac, Joanne Hartman, Mary Hill,
and the Write On Mamas